T0245746

DAVID

RITCHIE
CHARACTER
STUDY
SERIES

DAVID

C. MUNRO

RITCHIE

John Ritchie Publishing

40 Beansburn, Kilmarnock, Scotland

ISBN-13: 978 1 914273 21 6

Copyright © 2022 by John Ritchie Ltd.
40 Beansburn, Kilmarnock, Scotland

www.ritchiechristianmedia.co.uk

T ypeset by John Ritchie Ltd., Kilmarnock
Printed by Bell & Bain Ltd., Glasgow.

ABOUT THE AUTHOR

Craig Munro and his wife Hannah live in Fife, Scotland. They have three grown up children. Craig has been an elder in a local assembly, preacher and bible teacher for some time. He held senior national roles in education before being commended by the Glencraig Gospel Hall in 2016. He is active in the preaching of the gospel and teaching of the Word of God throughout the UK and other countries.

ACKNOWLEDGEMENT

Grateful thanks to Mr Iain Wilkie for proof-reading and editing the material submitted to him.

To my wife Hannah
who has helped me every step of the way
with this book and in life.

Contents

CHAPTER 1
David: His Character

Overview

David is one of the principal characters of our Bible. His name is mentioned over 1,000 times in Scripture, and it is the most referenced name in the Bible. In the New Testament his name comes immediately after that of the Lord Jesus: "The book of the generation of Jesus Christ, the son of David" (Matt 1:1). Interestingly, "David" is the second last name in the New Testament: "I am the root and offspring of David ... the grace of our Lord Jesus Christ be with you all. Amen" (Rev 22:16-21). In other words, David is a character who seems to shadow our blessed Lord and his life is full of meaning and lessons for all believers.

David as a picture of Christ

David, the son of Jesse, was born in Bethlehem, as was the Lord Jesus. When Christ was born, the angel said to Mary: "the Lord God shall give unto him the throne of his father David" (Luke 1:32). David is uniquely called by God, "a man after mine own heart" (Acts 13:22). Therefore, there are delightful features of David that remind us of the character of the Lord Jesus, and these will be brought out as we travel through the Scriptures with him. Furthermore, important prophecies concerning David in relation to Christ are still to be fulfilled: for example: "Behold, the days come, saith the LORD, that I will raise unto David a righteous Branch, and a King shall reign and prosper, and shall execute judgment and justice in the earth" (Jer 23:5). We are still waiting for our Lord to return to set up His Kingdom on earth, and in this context Ezekiel refers to Him as "David": "And I will set up one shepherd over them, and he shall feed them, even my servant David;

he shall feed them, and he shall be their shepherd" (Ezek 34:23). The covenant promise to David (2 Sam 7:8-17) is literally fulfilled in Christ and will know its ultimate fulfilment when He comes back to reign in this world.

Inspiration and comfort

David lived when King Saul was on the throne and the Philistines were Israel's major threat. David was a shepherd boy who became the King of Israel and ultimately removed the Philistine threat and established the Kingdom. It is an inspiring story of a young boy looking after sheep, who moves from poverty to prosperity by being catapulted into a position of authority from relative obscurity.

David knew real adversity. His psalms help us in days of trial, his prayers of penitence move us in our days of weakness and sin. His victory and valley experiences combine true devotion with real weakness encouraging all of us that we can do better, rise higher, and serve the Lord more valiantly.

Worship

David's psalms of worship touch the soul. The profundity and yet simplicity of David's words (as inspired by the Lord) are thrilling and so relevant to our experiences of life: "The Lord is my shepherd; I shall not want" (Ps 23:1); "The Lord is my light and my salvation; whom shall I fear?" (Ps 27:1); "The Lord is my rock, and my fortress" (Ps 18:2), to name but a few. David was devoted to his Lord and his worship draws us all nearer to the throne.

Warning

David made some major mistakes with tragic consequences, and we should learn from these so that we do not fall into the same errors. This book will follow the major movements in the life of David, reminding us that God can teach us in the dark days as well as at the high points in life. As we reflect upon David's sin, it encourages us to reflect on our lives. Our day of service will all soon be over, and we will have to give account of ourselves before God.

The first mention of David is found in the book of Ruth where we discover the intriguing story of his ancestry. The details of his life are found in First and Second Samuel (from 1 Samuel 16 onwards), in the early chapters of First Kings, and in First Chronicles. David is constantly referred to when the other kings of Judah are being discussed. He also wrote half the book of Psalms, and his name is found in almost all of the poetical books. His legacy is found in the exile accounts of Ezra and Nehemiah as well as in the Minor Prophets. The New Testament is saturated with references to him. Therefore, we will need to be selective in this pen portrait of David!

The broad movements of David's life are as:

• Shepherd boy (1 Samuel 16-17);

• Servant to King Saul in the palace, and ultimately son-in-law to the King (1 Samuel 18-20);

• Stranger and stateless man hounded by King Saul across the mountains and valleys of Judah (1 Samuel 21-2 Samuel 1);

• Sovereign on the throne of Judah and Israel (2 Samuel 2-1 Kings 2).

The base text used for this book will be 1 Samuel 16 to 1 Kings 2. The emphasis will be not so much in re-telling David's story, although some of that will be necessary, but rather in considering the lessons we can learn from the life of David for our lives today. Therefore, this book is devotional and practical in nature rather than being expository.

Thirteen of the titles of the 75 psalms of David share details of their settings, and these 13 psalms are all arranged chronologically in this book, after each chapter, without commentary, and after the relevant setting for each psalm has been discussed. If there is no psalm that we are aware of being written in the period under consideration, then a psalm has been selected that is relevant. It is hoped that the simple reading of the psalm in its context will prove to be a "selah" moment of deeper reflection upon the Word of God and appreciation of our God.

The chapters of this book can be summarised briefly.

Chapter 2   David: His Call   1 Samuel 16

This chapter describes how David is taken from looking after the sheep to be anointed king by the Prophet Samuel in front of all his brothers in Bethlehem. It impresses upon us the features that God is looking for in those whom He calls into His service.

Psalm 23 – a psalm probably written when David was a shepherd.

Chapter 3   David: His Courage   1 Samuel 17

This chapter tells of David's first and outstanding victory over the Philistine giant Goliath. It helps us, as we commence our Christian warfare, to realise that the giants in our life can be overcome.

Psalm 144 – a psalm written after a great victory.

Chapter 4   David: His Challenges   1 Samuel 18-19

David now moves from being a shepherd boy, to a soldier, to a servant of King Saul. These chapters outline how promotion into Saul's palace proves to be a poisoned chalice for David. Envy in the heart of King Saul because of David's victory over Goliath leads to him to seek David's demise. The challenges in the palace for David were greater than the Philistine challenge on the battlefield. Ultimately, David is forced to flee the palace. These chapters will help us realise that promotion can result in problems, and our greatest tests can be close to home and from the most unexpected sources. This section also deals with the importance of friendship, particularly when we are vulnerable, and the wise strategies that can prove effective to support saints in days of trial and difficulty.

Psalm 59 – a psalm written in this period when Saul sent soldiers to kill him, and they watched the house where he stayed with Michal.

Chapter 5   David: His Crisis   1 Samuel 20-21

These two chapters tell of the rejection of David as he goes from friend of King Saul to fugitive. We see David becoming stateless and a stranger. The crisis arrives, and the time comes for him to leave the palace. The subject should help us when God makes it clear that we must move on, and we face change in our lives. The mix of success and failure in the life of David's experience in the early days of being pursued is instructive. It is a reminder of the need to be careful when our life is being tested and when we enter periods of transition. It also shows us the attractive character of David and how, in the trials, convictions were formed which would be used in his future service as King. It is also a section that graphically details what true loyalty and friendship mean in a day of adversity.

Psalm 56- a psalm written when the Philistines took David at Gath (1 Sam 21).

Psalm 34 – a psalm written after David changed his behaviour before Abimelech, who drove him away, and he departed. It was probably penned in Adullam (1 Sam 21-22).

Chapter 6   David: His Cave   1 Samuel 22

These chapters show the fellowship David enjoyed as a fugitive in the cave of Adullam, and in the hold. It shows how fellowship can grow even in adversity.

Psalm 57 – a psalm written when David fled from Saul in the cave.

Psalm 142 – a psalm written by David as a prayer when he was in the cave.

Psalm 52 – a psalm written "when Doeg the Edomite came and told Saul, and said unto him, David is come to the house of Ahimelech".

Chapter 7   David: His Counsel   1 Samuel 23

This chapter teaches us lessons about David's intercession in times of persecution and God's counsel and guidance in his life. God instructs David to go and save the town of Keilah from the marauding forces of the Philistines, and then directs him to leave.

Psalm 54 – a psalm written at the end of 1 Samuel 23 "when the Ziphims came and said to Saul, Doth not David hide himself with us?".

Chapter 8   David: His Control   1 Samuel 24-26

These chapters show how David spared Saul twice from death, and Nabal the Carmelite from the sword through the instrumentality of Abigail. We learn that the sheathed sword is more powerful than the drawn one. This chapter reminds us of the need for meekness and patience to wait for God's will to come to fruition.

Psalm 63 - a psalm of David, when in the wilderness of Judah.

Psalm 116 – a psalm of preservation by David that could well have been written at this time.

Chapter 9   David: His Calamity   1 Samuel 27-30

David moves from the wilderness of Ziph back to being with Achish, the King of Gath. The relentless attacks of Saul seem to be affecting David's spiritual equilibrium. Fear can drive us to do things we know in our hearts are wrong. These next chapters describe how David seems to win the favour of the Philistine king to the extent that he is given Ziklag to live in. It is during this time, when David is with Achish, that the Amalekites come and remove all David's possessions and his people and burn Ziklag with fire. When we are not walking with the Lord there is no saying what losses we will incur. This section ends, however, with David "recovering all" and it has lessons for us on recovery in the life of the believer.

Psalm 4 – a psalm of David written after being preserved and restored "in distress".

Chapter 10   David: His Cry   I Samuel 31 - 2 Samuel 1

These chapters tell of the deaths of Saul and Jonathan at the hands of the Philistines, and David's response when he hears the tragic news. David learns of these events from an opportunistic Amalekite who adds various colourful details to the narrative, including the fact that he, the Amalekite, had killed Saul (2 Sam 1). David is deeply moved when he hears of their deaths, composing a funeral song of memorial to be taught to all the families in Israel. He feels keenly the loss in the kingdom. He slays the Amalekite for claiming to have killed Saul, showing at this moment that he is honourable and not seeking the throne for the throne's sake. Our true character will always be seen by how we react when our enemy is destroyed. The tenderness of David's heart is manifest, and his love for others is greater than any thought of self-advancement.

Psalm 18 – a psalm of David, "the servant of the LORD, who spake unto the LORD the words of this song in the day that the LORD delivered him from the hand of all his enemies, and from the hand of Saul".

Chapter 11   David: His Crowning   2 Samuel 2-5

These chapters detail how David is first crowned King of Judah and then eventually King over all Israel. It is a period in his life that deals with the dangers of transitions and teaches lessons regarding the type of leadership that is essential for effective rule.

Psalm 2 – a messianic psalm of David that looks forward to the King coming to reign.

Chapter 12   David: His Convictions   2 Samuel 6-8

This section sees David taking Zion, bringing the ark back to Jerusalem, and his deep conviction that God should have a House built for His glory. The revelation of the Davidic covenant with the promise of the Kingdom being established for ever is given here. God revealed that

He would establish David's household, and the House of God would be built in Jerusalem, initially by David's son. It reminds us of the crucial truth of the House of God and the centrality of God's House in His purposes. It is also the chapter where David expands the borders of the Kingdom and peace is established with neighbours.

Psalm 132 – a psalm that describes the movement of the Ark of the Covenant and David's desire ultimately to bring it to Jerusalem.

Psalm 60 – a psalm written by David at the time when the borders were being enlarged and when Joab returned and "smote of Edom in the valley of salt twelve thousand".

Chapter 13   David: His Compassion   2 Samuel 9-10

David is now settled in the Kingdom and his mind turns to those to whom he would like to show kindness. His choices illustrate his compassion and generous disposition. In 2 Samuel 9 he will show kindness to the offspring of King Saul, his former enemy, and in 2 Samuel 10 he will show kindness to Hanun the new king of Ammon, a group that had plagued God's people. In 2 Samuel 9 the kindness is surprising, and in 2 Samuel 10 the kindness is spurned as Hanun ridicules David's men who came to show sympathy at the time of his (Hanun's) father's death. This section provides important lessons about compassion and benevolence, and how we react when this is rejected.

Psalm 103 – a psalm where David is consumed with God's compassion to him.

Chapter 14   David: His Collapse   2 Samuel 11-13

These chapters deal with a terribly sad event in the life of David. David fails morally with Bathsheba and the repercussions are awful, moving from attraction to adultery to murder. The prophet Nathan is forced to tell him in no uncertain terms, "Thou art the man", and that God would avenge him fourfold. Around this point two of David's sons die - the child born to Bathsheba and his son Ammon who is killed by another of his sons, Absalom. The death of Absalom and Adonijah will follow in subsequent chapters. This section details how we can avoid falling into the same error, how sin leaves its impact but also provides hope in that forgiveness and restoration can be found with the Lord.

Psalm 51 - a psalm of David, when Nathan the prophet came unto him, after he had committed adultery with Bathsheba.

Chapter 15   David: His Curse   2 Samuel 14-19a

We now come to a most tragic time in the life of David. His own son, Absalom, ultimately hounds his father off the throne. Initially Absalom is in isolation after the death of Ammon. Joab intervenes to try to find a political solution and bring Absalom back to create a more normalised situation. The murder of Ammon by Absalom, however, is never dealt with, resulting in Absalom being given opportunity to promote himself and his own ideas. He grows in popularity and arrogance, then shows his true character by opposing his own father. By the time we reach chapter 16 he has usurped the throne, sent David into hiding across the Jordan, and callously raped the women of David's court publicly. Absalom is finally killed in war after his head was caught in a tree when he was on horseback, and he was then slain by Joab. The seven companions of David who helped him at this dreadful time provide lessons to us about how we can help others in a crisis.

Psalm 3 - a psalm of David, when he fled from Absalom his son.

Chapter 16   David: His Comeback   2 Samuel 19

Absalom is now dead. The attack is over. Getting back to "normal" for David should be easy! But is it? He does ultimately return to Jerusalem and the Kingdom is restored in this chapter, but the journey back is of interest to us. We hope to learn lessons of restoration from the friends that helped David back to the palace, and the barriers that require to be overcome for corporate unity to be restored.

Psalm 7 – a psalm of David, "which he sang unto the LORD, concerning the words of Cush the Benjamite" (probably Shimei).

Chapter 17   David: The Consequences of the Past   2 Samuel 20-21

In chapters 20 and 21 we read of unfinished business. Matters that should have been resolved years before now rear their heads again. In chapter 20 the old north/south division in the Kingdom, exacerbated by Sheba, needed to be healed and the relationship with Joab and David resolved. In chapter 21, the bones of Saul require to be buried, the sons of Goliath must be slain, and the legacy of sin against the Gibeonites by Saul needs to be judged. We learn in this section that our behaviour in the past has implications for the present, and matters need to be attended to. In Joab's case, his behaviour was not addressed, and this had to be resolved after David's reign. However, the usurpation of Sheba is quelled, the bones of past disputes are buried, and the Philistine aggression is removed. We will not read of Philistine threats toward Israel for many generations.

Psalm 139 – a psalm where David looks inwardly on himself and back over his life.

Chapter 18   David: The Cost of Counting   2 Samuel 23-24

Here we learn about true value. We have the names of the mighty men and some of the costly actions they took out of love for David. There are some surprising additions and omissions in the list of these mighty men. In chapter 24 we have the numbering of the army and the judgment that comes upon David and the people as result. The juxtaposition of the names of those who sacrificed for David along with the vexed issue of numbering is intriguing. God is interested not so much in numbers but in people that can be counted upon, that is, those who are reliable. The judgment that falls in chapter 24 reminds us of the cost of sin. The section ends with the purchase of the threshing floor of Araunah the Jebusite, for the House of God. The value of the House of God is underlined in these chapters. The very spot where Isaac was offered on the altar, Mount Moriah, is the place at which the Lord identified that His House was to be built.

Psalm 29 – a psalm written to the mighty about the might and strength of God.

Chapter 19   David: His Charge   1 Kings 1-2

David is now an old frail man who needs to be kept warm and nursed, but he still has incredible strength of faith. His forty-year reign is ending, and we see the anointing of Solomon at the King's command, and the solemn charge to Solomon by David. During this time, the rebellion by Adonijah is brought to a swift end. An orderly handover of power takes place while David is still alive. We learn in these sections about the importance of good transitions, the trials of old age, the blessings that an older generation can give us as well as the burdens that can be passed on intergenerationally.

Psalm 72 – a psalm for Solomon and a beautiful description of the climax of David's Kingdom in the person of Christ.

Chapter 20   David: His Contribution and Conclusion
1 Chronicles 23-29; 2 Samuel 22–23a

David gave Solomon a tremendous legacy for the House of God and the Word of God. The Chronicler lists for us the gold, silver, precious stones, priestly order, singers, instruments, and porters that David provided for the House of God. His wise sayings in these "last words" (2 Sam 23:1) are a reminder of David's vast contribution to the Word of God, for example his 75 psalms. Our own hearts are challenged as we review the life of David and see a man after God's own heart; a unique accolade for a remarkable man and an incredible life.

Psalm 30 – "A Psalm and Song at the dedication of the house of David", and a suitable doxology with which to end.

CHAPTER 2

David: His Call

1 Samuel 16

Staying Small

The account of the prophet Samuel coming to Bethlehem, the home of Jesse, to anoint one of his sons King of Israel is a story loved by Sunday School children through to the oldest believer. Seven of Jesse's sons are brought before Samuel to be considered as a candidate for the throne. All the sons, including the oldest Eliab, are visibly impressive (1 Sam 16:6). It is here we are taught one of the most important lessons in our Bible that God is not interested so much in externals but what is in the heart. Samuel is taught by God: "Look not on his countenance, or on the height of his stature; because I have refused him: for the LORD seeth not as man seeth; for man looketh on the outward appearance, but the LORD looketh on the heart" (1 Sam 16:7). God's selection criterion for service has not changed over time. The Lord Jesus warned the Pharisees that they were simply "whited sepulchres" (Matt 23:27). The Lord is still looking for moral and spiritual qualities in His people; He reads the heart.

Samuel surveys the seven boys twice (1 Sam 16:10) before asking Jesse if all his family are present. Jesse's reply is fascinating: "There remaineth yet the youngest, and, behold, he keepeth the sheep" (1 Sam 16:11). The word "youngest" means "least" (c.f. Jonah 3:5: "even to the least of them") or "insignificant". It is translated "small" (Ex 18:22: "'but every small matter they shall judge") or "little" (1 Sam 2:19: 'Moreover his mother made him a little coat"). We know that Jesse had eight sons (1 Sam 17:12) and that David was the seventh (1 Chron 2:15), but he may well have been the "least" in the pecking order of the family. Perhaps one of the boys died young as we only know the names of seven. He also had two sisters Zeruiah and Abigail (1 Chron 2:13-17). They were a lot older than him as their children Joab, Asahel etc were contemporaries of David (1 Sam 26:6; 2 Sam 2:18; 8:16). Certainly, David was the least likely in Jesse's eyes to be king, which is why the seven other boys are brought to Samuel, but David is left looking after the sheep. However, it was David that the Lord would point out to be anointed King (1 Sam 16:12). The lesson is simple: God loves to use the humble: "God hath chosen the weak things of the world to confound the things which are mighty" (1 Cor 1:27). If we feel overlooked and left out by others, then the life of David will inspire us to serve the Lord.

David's older brother Eliab, or Jesse (David's father), had asked him to look after the sheep when Samuel came. Not one of them thought that David should be there. Not one of them would have predicted that David would be king. Our language and our internal code of importance can be, sadly, no different to the world. Samuel initially looked at the height and good looks of the boys until the Lord told him not to do this. Does status matter to us? We often define ourselves by what we do for a living or what we are studying, or where we live. Let us remember that, like David, none of us are anything special in ourselves. The One whom we have come to love, the Lord Jesus, was also born in Bethlehem like David. Bethlehem is described as one of the smallest towns in Judah (Micah 5:2). He was brought up as a carpenter in Nazareth of which it was said: "Can there any good thing come out of Nazareth?" (John 1:46). Did He not stoop down and wash His disciples' feet (John 13)? The Lord Jesus took the lowest place and taught us a different way to think and live: "Let nothing be done through strife or vainglory; but in lowliness of mind let each esteem other better than themselves. Look not every man on his own things, but every man also on the things of others. Let this mind be in you, which was also in Christ Jesus: Who, being in the form of God, thought it not robbery to be equal with God ... made in the likeness of men ... even the death of the cross" (Phil 2:3-8).

It is not that David did not have any natural attributes. He did. David was red from outside work ("ruddy") and had pleasant eyes ("a beautiful countenance") which spoke of a good character as well as good looks (1 Sam 16:12). It was his character that fitted him to be king, as physical attributes fade and are only skin deep. The attributes of humility, courage, compassion, commitment, piety and purity are much more important than any physical beauty. Society today idolises the body, and the promotion of self has never been so blatantly encouraged. However, the Christian is not to be taken up with their own interests: we serve the Lord Christ. Just as David was content to look after the sheep under his charge we should seek to be in the pathway of the divine will and be content therein: "Godliness with contentment is great gain" (1 Tim 6:11); "Let every man abide in the same calling wherein he was called" (1 Cor 7:20). In David's case, the Lord chose to promote him and we see a practical outworking in his life of the proverb: "The fear of the LORD is the instruction of wisdom; and before honour is humility" (Prov 15:33). Peter wrote that Christians are to "be subject one to another, and be clothed with humility: for God resisteth the proud, and giveth grace to the humble" (1 Peter 5:5). Paul underscores this for us in the Roman epistle: "For I say, through the grace given unto me, to every man that is among you, not to think of himself more highly than he ought to think" (Rom 12:3). It is often in the ordinary that the extraordinary work for God appears. Rebekah was at the well doing what she would for any stranger, giving him and his camels water, unaware that she was answering the prayer of Abraham's servant and turning the wheel of history (Gen 24:14-21). May God gives us all help to keep small and do the ordinary well.

Singing

David was also known out in the fields for his singing and his playing of the harp. When King Saul was looking for a harpist one of his servants said: "Behold, I have seen a son of Jesse the Bethlehemite, that is cunning in playing, and a mighty valiant man, and a man of war, and prudent in matters, and a comely person, and the LORD is with him" (1 Sam 16:18). It is amazing that David's private devotions with the Lord when out with the sheep were noticed by others. Perhaps it was out in the fields that he composed Psalm 23. Thinking of himself as a shepherd and his care for the sheep undoubtedly caused David to reflect on Lord as his Shepherd and of His care for him. It was perhaps during this period that he composed Psalm 8 when gazing at the stars and the moon at night - "the work of thy fingers". He felt his own smallness and the magnitude and majesty of God. His intimate relationship with the beauty of nature - water, field, hill, forest, sun, moon, and stars permeate his psalms (Psalm 29; Psalm 8; Psalm 19, etc.). His life as a shepherd, working the sheep, exposed to wild beasts, and yet preserved by God amidst the green pastures and the still waters, furnishes imagery and colour to his psalms (Psalm 22:20-21; Psalm 23; Psalm 7:2). He sang and composed psalms alone and learned God in the secret place. When someone sings alone then it is not for show but for real. Our most authentic worship is when we are worshipping privately. Learning to be in awe of God in the secret place is our first calling as Christians. Later, David would worship in the House of God, but first he had to learn God alone.

Our private devotions influence the type of person we become. Worship moulds our character. The servant of Saul not only spoke about the skill of the harp-playing ("cunning in playing") of David, but his courage, strength and wisdom and his endearing nature. It was because of private devotions to God that David was enlisted in the public service of Saul to play the harp. What opportunities will be afforded to us in the public arena that are a direct result of knowing God privately?

Knowing God personally is life's biggest lesson. God can use worshippers. Worship is where it all starts. But worship must be in the Spirit (John 4:24). We learn in 1 Samuel 16 "that the Spirit of the Lord came upon David" (1 Sam 16:13). We need divine help to worship and cannot know God or appreciate Him but for the operation of the Holy Spirit in our lives. Worship is not the repetition of song lines, but a unique work of the Spirit of God in us. When David went to play the harp to Saul and sing, he learned that another spirit was at work in Saul – "an evil spirit" (1 Sam 16:23). There were some horrible nights of wind, rain and cold that David endured alone, but even in these days he saw the hand of God and was given strength to overcome.

Perhaps this equipped him in the difficult days with Saul. The trials of our lives can be part of God's plan for us to learn more about Him and equip us for future service (1 Sam 16:14).

People have physical, spiritual, and mental health problems; Saul clearly had these difficulties, and he is not unique. We might be used to help someone in circumstances like these. We can only help others in the measure we have been helped ourselves. David knew God's comfort (e.g. Psalm 23) in the solitude of Judah's pastureland, and he could bring this to the palace. When David sung and played his harp "Saul was refreshed" (1 Sam 16:23). We need people that can bring refreshment. May we try to sweeten the lives of others by our character and learn to sing with melodies in our heart! Paul clearly felt that our experiences of comfort in the past from the Lord are all with a view to cheering others: "Blessed be God, even the Father of our Lord Jesus Christ, the Father of mercies, and the God of all comfort; Who comforteth us in all our tribulation, that we may be able to comfort them which are in any trouble, by the comfort wherewith we ourselves are comforted of God" (2 Cor 1:3-4).

Finally, the harpist role that David takes up reminds us of divine guidance. Who would have thought that the shepherd boy would be taken from feeding sheep to the palace? The job description devised in the palace, however, was tailor-made for him (1 Sam 16:18). Even in difficult economic times we do not need to get too anxious about our future - God has a plan for our lives and can open doors in the most amazing of ways.

Shepherding

The first description of David by his father was that he was "with the sheep" (1 Sam 16:19). And we learn in 1 Samuel 17 that "David went and returned from Saul to feed his father's sheep at Bethlehem" (1 Sam 17:15). David loved the sheep.

It is very special that the early descriptions of David are as a shepherd. He followed in the footsteps of other great men of faith before him - for example, Joseph, Jacob, and Moses. David learned how to shepherd sheep before he shepherded men and women. Care for others becomes a hallmark of those who know God. Shepherding and supporting God's people will take on a new priority.

If there is one animal that needs cared for it is a sheep; they are different to lions or even wild ponies. Sheep have fleeces that need shorn, they get rag tail, foot rot, worms, and cannot defend themselves from predators. They need protected, they wander, and need fenced in at times and put in a fold at night. This is the illustration Scripture uses of humans – sheep: "all we like sheep have gone astray" (Isa 53:6). We stray and need support. We sometimes need "bottle fed" and all of us need the "green pasture" of Scripture to feed on. People who will be the shepherds in the assembly in the future will be doing the work of looking after sheep for many years before this, just as David learned with his father's sheep. We do not wake up one day and suddenly we are an elder or a shepherd. It is not a label but a labour, not a noun but a verb, not an office but a work. The choices that we make and the life that we live in our teens and twenties will determine who we are in our thirties, forties, fifties and older. God's people need to be confident of our care and character. They need to be able to trust us. They do not trust people that seek only place and position, but they trust people who serve. We must set our sails in the right direction in our youth. God's people require the best of food. "Feed the flock of God which is among you, taking the oversight thereof (or overseeing), not by constraint, but willingly; not for filthy lucre, but of a ready mind" (1 Peter 5:2). Shepherding is the response of love. The Saviour said to Peter: "Simon, son of Jonas, lovest thou me? He saith unto him, Yea, Lord; thou knowest that I love thee. He saith unto him, Feed my sheep" (John 21:16).

Now, whilst all this is specifically true for assembly shepherds, it is also true to say that all of us ought to be marked by love for the people of God: it is a divine commandment (1 John 3:23). The Lord Jesus had compassion on all the sheep: "And Jesus, when he came out, saw much people, and was moved with compassion toward them, because they were as sheep not having a shepherd: and he began to teach them many things" (Mark 6:34).

The early verses about David impress upon us his humility, his worship, and his dependability as a shepherd. These are the features that God will use in His service.

PSALM 23

[A Psalm of David.]

¹ The LORD is my shepherd; I shall not want.

² He maketh me to lie down in green pastures: he leadeth me beside the still waters.

³ He restoreth my soul: he leadeth me in the paths of righteousness for his name's sake.

⁴ Yea, though I walk through the valley of the shadow of death, I will fear no evil: for thou art with me; thy rod and thy staff they comfort me.

⁵ Thou preparest a table before me in the presence of mine enemies: thou anointest my head with oil; my cup runneth over.

⁶ Surely goodness and mercy shall follow me all the days of my life: and I will dwell in the house of the LORD for ever.

CHAPTER 3

David: His Courage

1 Samuel 17

The story of David and Goliath in 1 Samuel 17 is one of the best-known passages of the Bible. This account is more than a dramatic Sunday School story of big versus small or good supressing evil. It is the record of the early tests of David's faith and his courage in overcoming his enemies and even his own fears. It is the foundational chapter in the book of 1 Samuel and is a picture of the Lord Jesus descending into a greater valley than Elah, to destroy a larger giant than Goliath and "spoil his goods" at the cross of Calvary (Matt 12:28-29; Col 2:14-15). Furthermore, the chapter gives invaluable lessons of how we can also overcome giants in our own lives.

Learning how to slay giants

Learning how to slay the "giant" in our life is essential for each one of us. Each believer will face their own battles - what is a temptation to one may not be to another; what one saint fears greatly maybe quite different to the conflict facing another. Knowing the giant(s) in our lives is important.

There are only five individual giants named in Scripture, apart from Goliath's own family with four. The first giant in our Bible is Og. The only thing we know about him is his big bed (Deut 3:11). The bed would speak of apathy and immorality - a persistent problem for God's people. The next three giants are called Sheshai, Ahiman, and Talmai (Judges 1:10) and they lived in Hebron, meaning "the place of fellowship". This trinity of evil is still arrayed against the fellowship of God's people. They are the "men of a great stature" that made the spies feel like "grasshoppers" (Num 13:32-33). The giant of pride, which enlarges men, is still with us, creating hierarchies of religious orders and despising the simplicity, smallness and unsophisticated nature of the gatherings of the Lord's people. It takes a Caleb, that is someone with conviction for truth, who wholly follows the Lord, to destroy such (Josh 15:14). The last, and fifth, giant to be named is Goliath, the giant of despair. He made God's people weak with fear, but ultimately, he was defeated. This chapter has valuable lessons for us in our present-day circumstances.

Acknowledging God's greatness

Goliath is described in impressive detail: standing over 9 feet high (v 4) and daily hurling out his challenge for someone to fight him (vv 8-10). His armour is also described (vv 5-7): the 57kg coat of mail which he wore (5,000 shekels), the 7kg (600 shekels) spearhead, and the description of the shaft of his spear being "like a weaver's beam". These details show the sheer strength of this abnormally built man. His terrifying verbal assaults deflated the people of God (v 11). However, David is not discouraged. His eyes are on God and not Goliath. He calls God the "living God" (v 36), and "the Lord of hosts" and "the God of the armies of Israel" (v 45). David will eventually speak directly to Goliath saying: "Thou comest to me with a sword, and with a spear, and with a shield: but I come to thee in the name of the LORD of hosts, the God of the armies of Israel, whom thou hast defied" (v.45). When we see God's vastness and power then no enemy will be too great to be overcome. John could encourage us: "greater is he that is in you, than he that is in the world" (1 John 4:4), and Paul underscores this: "What shall we then say to these things? If God be for us, who can be against us?" (Rom 8:31).

Seeing the enemy from God's standpoint

We get two views of Goliath. His physicality and verbal dexterity are described in 1 Samuel 17:4-11, and his vulnerability and culpability are described in verses 36-37. David calls Goliath an "uncircumcised

Philistine" not a giant, but one who had defied the "armies of the living God" (v 26). We too have huge enemies arrayed against us. Paul speaks of "spiritual wickedness in high places" and the "rulers of the darkness of this world" (Eph 6:12). It is good to know that the Lord Jesus in His death stripped principalities and powers of their glory: "And having spoiled principalities and powers, he made a shew of them openly, triumphing over them in it" (Col 2:15). We need to see the big enemies in our lives as already defeated foes if we are to know what it is to overcome them, practically on a daily basis.

Goliath is a Philistine. The Philistines came from Egypt, the old name of which was Mizraim (Gen 10:13-14). They were a sea-faring people, who worshipped the fish-faced god Dagon (Judges 16:23). They crossed the Mediterranean into Caphtor (Cyprus – Amos 9:7). They then came into the coastal region of Israel, the Gaza area. They inhabited divine territory, but they had never been redeemed. They are a picture of the world in the church. They were, as Goliath exhibited, ruthless and rude and had no interest in divine truth. They had iron chariots (Judges 1:9; Joshua 17:18) and big armies (1 Sam 13:5) and created systems that were hard to break down but easy to be replicated. The Philistine attitude today will attack the inspiration of Scripture, the cardinal truths, for example, the deity of Christ or his bodily resurrection, and will use worldly ideas for controlling church practice. Goliath is not only the giant of fear but the giant of secularity in divine things. His strategies are alive today and must be destroyed by successive generations of God's people.

Building confidence from past victories

We do not go out and slay Goliath-like giants every day. It starts normally with something smaller. In David's case he had killed a lion and a bear before he ever slew the giant Goliath and it is this that gives him confidence: "The LORD that delivered me out of the paw of the lion, and out of the paw of the bear, he will deliver me out of the hand of this Philistine. And Saul said unto David, Go, and the LORD be with thee" (1 Sam 17:37). We need victory over smaller enemies in our life;

little victories over barriers to spiritual progress leads to increasing confidence that bigger enemies can be taken, and more ground can be captured for the Lord. It is good to keep a prayer record of answered prayers and of victories in the service of God. We need to ask the Lord for strength in every circumstance and be determined by the grace of God to overcome any sin or other "giant" in our lives. Our Lord has triumphed over the strong man, and in so doing can strengthen us: "These things I have spoken unto you, that in me ye might have peace. In the world ye shall have tribulation: but be of good cheer; I have overcome the world" (John 16:33).

Using what we have to our hand

David used the sling in his hand to slay the giant: "his sling was in his hand: and he drew near to the Philistine" (1 Sam 17:40). He used what was to his hand and what he had proved before. David had learned how to manipulate the sling in the quiet place when wild animals came to destroy his lambs. He says in Psalm 144 that God taught him how to use it, and it was God that he depended upon: "Blessed be the LORD my strength, which teacheth my hands to war, and my fingers to fight" (Ps 144:1-2). Whether it was Moses with his staff, Samson with his ass's jawbone, or Jael with her tent pin and hammer, they all used what they had to their hand to do the service of God. God wants us to take what He has given us from Scripture and work with it. The Lord will not ask us to cross the sea on mission work if we have never crossed our own street to reach our neighbours for Christ. He wants us to work with what is next to us. Moses was asked by God: "What is that in thine hand?" (Ex 4:2). We all need to answer this question.

Using only what we have proved previously

Saul tries to arm David with a coat of mail and a helmet of brass from his own armoury, but David had not proved these and so he refused them, sticking to the sling in which he had confidence from the past (1 Sam 17:38-39). We do not need something innovative, like a Bible College diploma, to serve the Lord. The simple testimony of the blind man when the Lord Jesus was on earth had a huge impact: "one thing I know, that, whereas I was blind, now I see" (John 9:25). We need nothing more than our testimony in God's Word. David was simply equipped for Goliath, but he was surely and fully equipped: "Then he took his staff in his hand; and he chose for himself five smooth stones from the brook, and put them in a shepherd's bag, in a pouch (scrip) which he had, and his sling was in his hand. And he drew near to the Philistine" (1 Sam 17:40 NKJV). The Scriptures are seen in picture form in the sling to slay, the staff to give support, the scrip to store, and the five smooth stones to strike. The humble saint armed with God's Word is fully equipped for every giant.

David will come with a sling in humble dependence on God. David had already been prepared to be the message boy (bringing bread to his brothers and cheese to their captains, 1 Sam 17:17-18) before ever God used him to be the man to fight Goliath. We need to be prepared to do the menial tasks amongst God's people first. Our Lord Himself took the towel and washed His disciples' feet. His ministry teaches us that we are here to serve, and not to be served.

Five stones were taken from the brook but only one was required. There are five giants actually named in Scripture. As already noted, Goliath himself had four sons (2 Sam 21:15-22), and so possibly all five giants were there, hence the reasons for the five stones. The enemy always comes in fives – see the five kings of Midian (Num 31:8), the five kings of the Amorites (Josh 10:5), and the five lords of the Philistines (Josh 13:3) that Israel had to defeat as they came into the land. We too have enemies in fives: "Wherefore laying aside all malice, and all guile, and hypocrisies, and envies, and all evil speakings ..." (1 Peter 2:1). Just as the great image of Nebuchadnezzar came crashing down through one stone (Dan 2:34) so the great giants of our lives can be defeated through the direct application of God's Word. The power lies in the Word

Ignoring distraction

When giants are being slain distraction can come from the most unexpected sources. In David's case his brother Eliab, not the Philistines, was a major interference. He seems angry with David for having spiritual thoughts: "Eliab's anger was kindled against David, and he said, Why camest thou down hither? and with whom hast thou left those few sheep in the wilderness? I know thy pride, and the naughtiness of thine heart; for thou art come down that thou mightest see the battle. And David said, What have I now done? Is there not a cause?" (1 Sam 17:28-29). Eliab thinks he can judge David's motives – he claims David is "all talk" and merely an immature spectator who wants to see a battle but has no idea of the consequences of his words. David does not take Eliab on and seek to explain his motives to him, but simply states that he has done nothing wrong and there is a huge cause at stake – the honour of God and His people. "A soft answer turns away wrath" (Prov 15:1) is wise advice in such circumstances.

Saul, too, was a distraction to David. Saul's words were not aimed at David's immaturity but at David's apparent inexperience and possible incompetence against such a mighty warrior: "Thou art not able to go against this Philistine to fight with him: for thou art but a youth, and he a man of war from his youth". Once again David dismissed these words and did not allow them to weaken him saying, "Let no man's heart fail because of him; thy servant will go and fight with this Philistine" (1 Sam 17:32-33). Saul then gives David misdirected advice about what we must wear. Again, this was dismissed by David. We will all have to face people who doubt our abilities and attributes for the service of the Lord and can insult us (sometimes unknowingly) and give us faulty advice. We must listen to godly counsel, and if we are always moving with no-one seeing God's hand with us then there is a problem. However, it is also true that we will face opposition, sadly sometimes from other believers. We must recognise that when we know we are found in the will of God nothing will weaken our resolve.

Finally, Goliath moves toward David with his shield bearer in front of him, disdains his youth-like appearance, and questions his sanity in coming to him "with staves". He curses David by his gods and tells him that he will feed him to the birds (1 Sam 17:41-44). We can be affected by the words of our enemies and their ideas can register and weaken us just at the very jaws of triumph. But David kept his eye on God and spoke these extraordinary words: "Thou comest to me with a sword, and with a spear, and with a shield: but I come to thee in the name of the LORD of hosts, the God of the armies of Israel, whom thou hast defied. This day will the LORD deliver thee into mine hand; and I will smite thee, and take thine head from thee; and I will give the carcases of the host of the Philistines this day unto the fowls of the air, and to the wild beasts of the earth; that all the earth may know that there is a God in Israel. And all this assembly shall know that the LORD saveth not with sword and spear: for the battle is the LORD'S, and he will give you into our hands" (1 Sam 17:45-47).

The lesson surely is this. When we keep looking up, nothing can distract us. The battle is the Lord's. Like Asa we say, "...we rest on thee and in thy name we go" (2 Chron 14:11).

Involving others in our victories

The final lesson in slaying our giants is to acknowledge God and the role played by others. These verses show that David involved all Israel in the victory, even although he fired the stone which struck Goliath on the forehead, bringing him down to the ground before using Goliath's own sword to remove his head (1 Sam 17:48-51). The Philistine armies flee in fear and Saul's army, emboldened by David's triumph, follow after them and complete the victory: "And the men of Israel and of Judah arose, and shouted, and pursued the Philistines, until thou come to the valley, and to the gates of Ekron. And the wounded of the Philistines fell down by the way to Shaaraim, even unto Gath, and unto Ekron. And the children of Israel returned from chasing after the Philistines, and they spoiled their tents" (1 Sam 17:52-53). David returns to his own tent as one of the soldiers (v 54). A generosity of spirit, and a collective responsibility in the days of our triumph is essential if we are to know ultimate victory. It was only because all Israel were involved that the Philistines were completely beaten, and the threat removed. When God saves a precious soul, for example, it is important to acknowledge that no matter what role God has given us in this process we are only links in a long chain, and that it is God alone who saves.

God did not forget David's bravery. Saul asks Abner to make further enquiry about David's family background. Although Saul knew him as his harpist, he did not know the full family context, and they are about to be given the "freedom" of the country (1 Sam 17:25). David is brought by Abner to Saul and David becomes an employee of the Royal Court in Saul's palace (1 Sam 17:55-58; 18:2). We, too, must realise that giving all the glory to God when God is blessing us, and being generous by acknowledging the role that others are playing, is of vital importance. It is this that gives confidence to people, especially if we are given increasing leadership roles within the assembly. God will always honour such an approach.

Conclusion

This chapter is left in our Bibles to encourage us. God's people face many challenges from intellectual attacks on our faith, to group pressure of colleagues at work or school, or the fear of major health problems. The internal giants of pride and lust are a constant pressure, and the ogres of carnality and materialism must be faced and destroyed. If a simple shepherd boy with a sling and a stone can slay Goliath, so the simplest saint armed with God's Word can overcome the biggest of enemies. Our Lord Jesus defeated the "strong man" at Calvary and has given us the Spirit of God to overcome the enemy in our lives (Heb 2:14-15). John says of a group of believers in the end times: "And they overcame him by the blood of the Lamb, and by the word of their testimony" (Rev 12:11). We too can be "overcomers" through the Word of the Lord Jesus and His work on the cross.

PSALM 144

[A Psalm of David.]

¹ Blessed be the LORD my strength, which teacheth my hands to war, and my fingers to fight:

² My goodness, and my fortress; my high tower, and my deliverer; my shield, and he in whom I trust; who subdueth my people under me.

³ LORD, what is man, that thou takest knowledge of him! or the son of man, that thou makest account of him!

⁴ Man is like to vanity: his days are as a shadow that passeth away.

⁵ Bow thy heavens, O LORD, and come down: touch the mountains, and they shall smoke.

⁶ Cast forth lightning, and scatter them: shoot out thine arrows, and destroy them.

⁷ Send thine hand from above; rid me, and deliver me out of great waters, from the hand of strange children;

⁸ Whose mouth speaketh vanity, and their right hand is a right hand of falsehood.

⁹ I will sing a new song unto thee, O God: upon a psaltery and an instrument of ten strings will I sing praises unto thee.

¹⁰ It is he that giveth salvation unto kings: who delivereth David his servant from the hurtful sword.

¹¹ Rid me, and deliver me from the hand of strange children, whose mouth speaketh vanity, and their right hand is a right hand of falsehood:

¹² That our sons may be as plants grown up in their youth; that our daughters may be as corner stones, polished after the similitude of a palace:

¹³ That our garners may be full, affording all manner of store: that our sheep may bring forth thousands and ten thousands in our streets:

¹⁴ That our oxen may be strong to labour; that there be no breaking in, nor going out; that there be no complaining in our streets.

¹⁵ Happy is that people, that is in such a case: yea, happy is that people, whose God is the LORD.

CHAPTER 4

David: His Challenges

1 Samuel 18-19

David now moves from being a shepherd boy, to a soldier, to a servant of King Saul. These chapters outline how promotion into Saul's palace proves to be a poisoned chalice for David. Envy in the heart of King Saul because of David's victory over Goliath leads him to seek David's demise. The challenges in the palace for David were greater than the Philistine challenge on the battlefield. Ultimately, David is forced to flee the palace. These chapters will help us realise that promotion can result in problems, and our greatest tests can be close to home and from the most unexpected sources. This section also deals with the importance of friendship, particularly when we are vulnerable, and the wise strategies that can prove effective to support saints in days of trial and difficulty.

CHAPTER 18

If in 1 Samuel 16 we are taught humility from David, and in 1 Samuel 17 we are taught courage, then 1 Samuel 18 teaches us how to be wise, particularly when we are the target of envy.

Discernment

After David has destroyed Goliath, Saul takes him into the palace to serve him on a permanent basis (1 Sam 18:2). David displays real wisdom in the way he conducts himself in the palace and Saul promotes him over the army: "And David went out whithersoever Saul sent him, and behaved himself wisely: and Saul set him over the men of war, and he was accepted in the sight of all the people, and also in the sight of Saul's servants" (1 Sam 18:5). Promotion can sometimes make us less humble and less able to reach the people around us. But David's wisdom was not just noticed by the "top brass" in Saul's court; all the people loved David! It is good when our heavenly wisdom is acknowledged in the world. Paul recognised the importance of this, saying, "Walk in wisdom toward them that are without, redeeming the time" (Col 4:5).

Ditty

A lack of wisdom is shown by the women in this chapter. David is returning with King Saul from another victory over Israel's enemies, and the people begin to dance and shout and with their musical instruments they sing: "Saul hath slain his thousands, and David his ten thousands" (1 Sam 18:7). We should be aware of how elaborate public praise can have drastic effects upon people, especially those who have a propensity to jealousy. We should try not to compare people in public. This song of the women infuriated King Saul and envy entered deep into his heart: "And Saul was very wroth, and the saying displeased him; and he said, They have ascribed unto David ten thousands, and to me they have ascribed but thousands: and what can he have more but the kingdom? And Saul eyed David from that day and forward" (1 Sam 18:8-9). Many big problems start off as a "little ditty"; something silly, something trivial, something unwise. The remaining chapters in 1 Samuel (chapters 18-31) show how the green-eyed monster of envy resulted in Saul behaving like an animal; ultimately to his tragic downfall. We find him near the end of the book consulting a witch instead of God! Solomon would have been told about it by David. Solomon knew that envy eats away inside us like cancer and wrote in his proverbs: "A sound heart is the life of the flesh: but envy the rottenness of the bones" (Prov 14:30). Envy is the pain we feel within us when someone achieves or receives what we think rightly belongs to us. It can lead to outrageous behaviour: "Wrath is cruel, and anger is outrageous; but who is able to stand before envy?" (Prov 27:4). Whatever unwise statements people make it is still never right for us to act in a jealous manner. We need to remember that unchecked envy grows and pushes us down paths where it is very hard to carry out a U-turn. We need to be sensitive to sin in our life as we do not know where unjudged sin leads.

There are four strategies in the palace which were used to try to bring David down and trip him up:

- Direct attack   - wisdom in evasion
- Demotion   - wisdom in demotion
- Damaged heart   - wisdom in emotion
- Dangerous task   - wisdom in diversion.

Direct attack

The day after this song has been sung David is taking the place of submission to Saul and playing the harp to him in the palace when an evil spirit is permitted by the Lord to remain on King Saul, and in a fit of envy he throws a javelin at David to pin him to the wall. He fails and tries again. On both occasions it misses (1 Kings 18:10-11). How many near misses have we had in our lives? Sometimes these near misses have been of our own making, other times by people who should know better. The Psalmist could exclaim: "But as for me, my feet were almost gone; my steps had well-nigh slipped" (Ps 73:2) and again, "Blessed is that man that maketh the LORD his trust" (Ps 40:4). Truly we can all say: "It is of the LORD'S mercies that we are not consumed, because his compassions fail not. They are new every morning: great is thy faithfulness" (Lam 3:22-23). We may never know, this side of glory, how many arrows were diverted by the Lord that had been aimed at us by the Evil One.

David's wisdom was seen in his evasion. Sometimes we have to flee: "Wherefore, my dearly beloved, flee from idolatry" (1 Cor 10:14). We need to know when to flee and when to fight. In Iconium Paul fled (Acts 14:6) as they sought to stone him, but in Antioch he stayed (Acts

13:14-52). Later David would rise even higher, as with incredible meekness he handed the spear back to Saul (1 Sam 26:22), but here he feels his own vulnerability and chooses to escape. It is good to know our own weaknesses. We take comfort in the fact that "There hath no temptation taken you but such as is common to man: but God is faithful, who will not suffer you to be tempted above that ye are able; but will with the temptation also make a way to escape, that ye may be able to bear it" (1 Cor 10:13).

Demotion

When direct attack fails to change David, Saul demotes him to be in charge of 1,000 men rather than a whole army, and we learn that Saul is afraid of David because he knows the Lord is with him. Interestingly, we learn that David still acts prudently even although he is demoted and grows in favour with the people: "Therefore Saul removed him from him, and made him his captain over a thousand; and he went out and came in before the people. And David behaved himself wisely in all his ways; and the LORD was with him. Wherefore when Saul saw that he behaved himself very wisely, he was afraid of him. But all Israel and Judah loved David, because he went out and came in before them" (1 Sam 18:13-16). Perhaps we can all learn lessons of the importance of prudent behaviour even if our employer envies us, directly attacks us, or demotes us. The world can see the reality of our faith when we do not grumble like everyone else, even more so when our salary is reduced, or our position of authority is removed. Paul instructs the believers in Colosse along the same lines, and they lived in a day of slavery. These words are pertinent to our employment today and to jobs in the assembly or voluntary work in the community: "Servants, obey in all things your masters according to the flesh; not with eye-service, as men pleasers; but in singleness of heart, fearing God: And whatsoever ye do, do it heartily, as to the Lord, and not unto men; Knowing that of the Lord ye shall receive the reward of the inheritance: for ye serve the Lord Christ. But he that doeth wrong shall receive for the wrong which he hath done: and there is no respect of persons" (Col 3:22-25). This is not easy, but by God's grace it can be done. Jacob did this before Laban when his wages were changed ten times (Gen 31:7). Joseph was wrongly accused by Potiphar and thrown out of his job and into prison yet still conducted himself in a way that gained the favour of the keeper of the prison, for "the Lord was with him" (Gen 39:20-23). What an opportunity we have, like David, to testify in our occupations to those who do not know the Lord Jesus.

Damaged heart

Saul is not finished; he tries to damage David's heart. If he cannot destroy him physically, he will ruin him mentally or morally. He promised him his daughter as a wife and then when the time came for the wedding, he gave her to another man. The Proverbs say: "Hope deferred maketh the heart sick" (Prov 13:12). Many a Christian who has been able to hold their own with intellectual challenges on Scripture, or even physical opposition for the cause of Christ, have stumbled when it comes to the "matters of the heart". Deliberately playing around with other people's emotions is wicked. David seems to pass the test at this point, but he will be tried again on his emotions and affections.

Our challenge might not be the promise of a wife but the promise of promotion or an inheritance or something else and then, just when it is almost ours, it is cruelly taken away. The Proverbs have good advice here: "Keep thy heart with all diligence; for out of it are the issues of life" (Prov 4:23). We must watch who or what we give our heart to!

Dangerous task

Saul discovers that his other daughter Michal is in love with David and chooses to exploit this situation. He offers David his daughter in marriage knowing that David would never be able to afford the bride-price. Instead, Saul makes the dowry he requires to be one hundred Philistine foreskins. He is trying to set an unobtainable goal for David by dangling before him the privilege of a place in the royal family but placing him in severe danger with a view to his being killed. David initially refuses but then sees an opportunity to destroy the enemy of God's people and so slays 200 Philistines for Saul and marries Michal, Saul's daughter. Saul is afraid and hates David even more but we read that: "David behaved himself more wisely than all the servants of Saul; so that his name was much set by" (1 Sam 18:29-30).

We will learn that people will play with our hearts, and they may set unobtainable goals for us with the promise of material reward. Many of God's people are in careers where they are locked into this type of practice. We need grace to be true to our Lord and act wisely. It is good to consider what we are chasing and wanting from our employment. Are we being diverted from the real and important issues? The time may come, like David, where a change in employment is necessary to maintain Christian integrity. The challenge of killing Philistines is deliberate by Saul – setting before David what appears to be a spiritual task (killing the enemy of the Lord's people) for carnal gain. The work of God never promises material reward. Any "gospel" that promises material prosperity for spiritual activity is a false gospel and is warned about by Paul to Timothy (2 Tim 3:1-7).

Conclusion

David displays wisdom despite direct physical attack, demotion from his position of employment, a damaged heart through false hope of marriage, and being diverted into dangerous tasks set in exchange for incredible reward. David is learning that avoiding javelins in the palace is harder work than slaying giants in the battlefield. David is not now facing the giant of fear in Goliath but the giant of envy in Saul. We too must learn that success today does not mean triumph tomorrow. *This* giant he will ultimately have to run away from and not fight, just as Joseph ran from the giant of lust in Potiphar's wife (Gen 39). Paul says that there are some things we must run from - for example, "Flee fornication" (1 Cor 6:18). Promotion and prosperity can sometimes lead to a greater test than poverty and adversity just as David found in moving from shepherd boy to serving in the palace.

CHAPTER 19

Protection

If 1 Samuel 18 is the pursuit of David by Saul, then chapter 19 is the protection of David by his friends. In 1 Samuel 18 we learn the strategies of our enemies to derail us spiritually, in chapter 19 we learn strategies for helping to protect others who are under attack.

Friends are crucial when we are facing adversity. Saul wanted to kill David (1 Sam 19:1) and told his son Jonathan of his intentions. Jonathan, however, proves to be a true friend to David: "the soul of Jonathan was knit with the soul of David, and Jonathan loved him as his own soul" (1 Sam 18:1). He had already given his robe and his sword, bow and girdle to David after his victory over Goliath (1 Sam 18:4). It must have aggravated Saul that Jonathan saw in David the true King, accepting that he himself would not inherit the throne after his father. At least this is what Jonathan says to David in 1 Samuel 23:16-17. It is wonderful when we can recognise true greatness in another and let them know. To tell someone else that they are better at doing something than we are, is a sign of true greatness. This is particularly poignant when we remember that Jonathan was significantly older than David and would have been more experienced than David for the throne.

Three strategies are used to protect and preserve David by Jonathan, Michal, and Samuel: Intervention, Intrigue, and Intercession.

Intervention of Jonathan (vv 1-10)

David is fleeing for his life from Saul, and Jonathan asks David to hide himself in a certain place and wait. Jonathan then talks directly to his father with David overhearing the conversation. We are permitted to listen into to what he says. He speaks of the character of David. He is factually accurate but warm. He reminds his father that David has always been faithful to him as King, that he had put his neck on the line for the nation when he took on Goliath, and argues that there is no cause to be against him. He was tactful and did not mention David's popularity with the people. We need to be wise when handling sensitive situations. This intervention seems to work, albeit temporarily. Saul swears that he will do David no harm, and David is restored to his position before the King. It is good when those we respect begin to act as peacemakers and seek to intervene to avoid casualties and major collateral damage, especially when individuals begin to behave badly and crush good people. The Lord Jesus said, "Blessed are the peacemakers" (Matt 5:9). This will need tact, diplomacy and courage. Pauls says: "... walk worthy of the vocation wherewith ye are called, With all lowliness and meekness, with longsuffering, forbearing one another in love; Endeavouring to keep the unity of the Spirit in the bond of peace" (Eph 4:1-3). We should go out of our way to help people to behave in a Christ-like manner and aim to be a Jonathan.

Intrigue and intuition of Michal (vv 11-17)

However, the effect of this helpful intervention by Jonathan is short lived, for as soon as David is successful after another victory over the Philistines envy erupts again and Saul, for the third time, throws a javelin at David. Once again, he misses. This time Michal, David's wife, is key to David's being preserved. She warns him he must flee for his life and lets him down through the window to escape from the house. He did not know this then, but he would not return for over ten years. We little know how important acts of kindness are to each other. Today's kind act might be our last opportunity. David wrote a Psalm about it afterwards (Psalm 59). Years later, Paul would be let down through a window to escape from the hatred of the Jews and he did not forget it either (2 Cor 11:33). Michal hatches an ingenious plan to hide a life-size image in the bed, and when Saul's soldiers arrive to arrest him, she tells them that David is in bed sick, so buying time for David to run away. Sometimes those close to us do things to protect us in ways that we cannot condone. Michal's lies were not necessary and only caused her to tell even more lies to her father Saul, to the point of blaming David. Michal's life-size image begs the question about her own idolatry, but God still blessed her desire to protect David's life. If God could use Pharaoh in Egypt to feed his people in a time of famine in Joseph's Day without in any way condoning the pagan practices of Egypt, then He could use Michal to protect David without approving of her methods. God blesses Michal for simply wanting to do right by David and he still blesses people today who want to do right by God's people. Similar truth is seen in the life of Rahab when she hid the spies (Joshua 2).

Intercession of Samuel (vv 18-24)

The prophet Samuel is now instrumental in preserving David. Saul pursues David and David runs to Samuel in Naioth in Ramah. Saul sends three bands of soldiers to arrest David but the holiness of the man of God seems to affect them all as they begin to prophesy, meaning they sang songs of praise. Saul then arrives to take David himself and when he comes into Samuel's presence seeking David, Saul too begins prophesying and is unable to succeed in capturing and killing David. God has ways to humble the most angry and wicked of people. Indeed, Scripture says: "surely the wrath of man shall praise thee" (Ps 76:10).

All three people in different ways helped David: Jonathan through spiritual intervention, Michal through intrigue and intuition, and Samuel by intercession. We need people who are prepared to help God's people – by promoting and advocating like Jonathan, by pushing open windows of opportunity for others like Michal, by praying like Samuel. Working for others is our Christian calling: "Look not every man on his own things, but every man also on the things of others" (Phil 2:4); "Bear ye one another's burdens, and so fulfil the law of Christ" (Gal 6:2).

Samuel's prayer and intercession is the hardest approach but is available to us all. How we need to appreciate the power of prayer. Out of the three interventions prayer was the most effective. In the other two methods, Saul was turned back or thwarted from his purpose, but in the last one Saul himself begins to pray and praise. Whilst Jonathan's intercession worked once, and Michal's window trick worked once, neither was likely to have worked a second time. But prayer worked four times in a row – stopping three separate bands of soldiers and Saul himself. Paul knew the power of prayer and knew how effective it was time and again: "For the weapons of our warfare are not carnal, but mighty through God to the pulling down of strong holds" (2 Cor 10:4). Like David, he had been delivered many times by those who prayed, and that is why he exhorts: "Pray without ceasing" (1 Thess 5:17). The influence of a godly Samuel was the main reason why the prayer was effective here: "The effectual fervent prayer of a righteous man availeth much" (James 5:16). May we be inspired to be a Samuel.

PSALM 59

[To the chief Musician, Altaschith, Michtam of David; when Saul
sent, and they watched the house to kill him.]

¹ Deliver me from mine enemies, O my God: defend me from them that rise up against me.

² Deliver me from the workers of iniquity, and save me from bloody men.

³ For, lo, they lie in wait for my soul: the mighty are gathered against me; not for my transgression, nor for my sin, O LORD.

⁴ They run and prepare themselves without my fault: awake to help me, and behold.

⁵ Thou therefore, O LORD God of hosts, the God of Israel, awake to visit all the heathen: be not merciful to any wicked transgressors. Selah.

⁶ They return at evening: they make a noise like a dog, and go round about the city.

⁷ Behold, they belch out with their mouth: swords are in their lips: for who, say they, doth hear?

⁸ But thou, O LORD, shalt laugh at them; thou shalt have all the heathen in derision.

⁹ Because of his strength will I wait upon thee: for God is my defence.

¹⁰ The God of my mercy shall prevent me: God shall let me see my desire upon mine enemies.

¹¹ Slay them not, lest my people forget: scatter them by thy power; and bring them down, O Lord our shield.

¹² For the sin of their mouth and the words of their lips let them even be taken in their pride: and for cursing and lying which they speak.

¹³ Consume them in wrath, consume them, that they may not be: and let them know that God ruleth in Jacob unto the ends of the earth. Selah.

¹⁴ And at evening let them return; and let them make a noise like a dog, and go round about the city.

¹⁵ Let them wander up and down for meat, and grudge if they be not satisfied.

¹⁶ But I will sing of thy power; yea, I will sing aloud of thy mercy in the morning: for thou hast been my defence and refuge in the day of my trouble.

¹⁷ Unto thee, O my strength, will I sing: for God is my defence, and the God of my mercy.

CHAPTER 5

David: His Crisis

1 Samuel 20-21

Chapters 20 and 21 describe the rejection of David as he goes from friend of King Saul to fugitive. We have seen David and his call from being a shepherd boy (1 Sam 16), his courage as a soldier to defeat Goliath (1 Sam 17), and his challenge in the palace as the servant and son-in-law of King Saul (1 Sam 18-19). We will now look at David becoming stateless and a stranger. The crisis arrives here, and the time comes for him to leave the palace. The subject should help us when God makes it clear that we must move on, and we face change in our lives. The mix of success and failure in the life of David's experience in the early days of being pursued is instructive. It is a reminder of the need to be careful when our life is being tested and when we enter periods of transition. It also shows us the attractive character of David and how, in the trials, convictions were formed which would be used in his future service as King. It is also a section that graphically details what true loyalty and friendship mean in a day of adversity.

CHAPTER 20

In 1 Samuel 18 we saw the tactics the world can use to derail the believer and, in chapter 19, how they can be overcome. In this section we want to consider the difficult but essential decisions we must make to leave systems like Saul's palace that are carnal. In 1 Samuel 20 David is weighing everything up and the Lord directs him to go in no uncertain fashion. The chapter may be broken up as follows:

- The field - hatching the plan: vv 1-23

- The feast - gauging reaction: vv 24-34
- The firing of the arrows - signalling final separation: vv 35-42.

The field (vv 1-23)

David needs to know how the Lord is directing him. Should he return to the palace or not? His sense of duty tells him he should stay in the palace serving the king, but the direct attacks upon him by Saul tell David that he would be foolish to do so. He says to Jonathan that, "there is but a step between me and death" (v 3). Jonathan thinks his father would not kill David, despite all the evidence to the contrary. We sometimes wonder how Jonathan could possibly think like this, but loyalty can blind us to simple facts. Both David and Jonathan needed a clear word from the Lord.

Together they hatch a plan to will find out for sure what Saul's intentions are, and what the will of God is for David. During their planning they make a covenant with one another that if David has to flee he will remember Jonathan and not cut off the family of Saul in the future when he is King (vv 1-23). David never forgot this promise when he was placed on the throne – his love and loyalty to Mephibosheth, Saul's grandson, was exemplary (2 Sam 9).

The plan they agree is simple. David will go into hiding and on the third day he will return to the place, near the rock Ezel, a place where he had hidden himself before when Jonathan had spoken up for David to Saul, as recorded in the first few verses of 1 Samuel 19. Jonathan, on the other hand, will go to the monthly feast and David's absence will be noticed. Jonathan would then have opportunity to discuss David's position with his father and he would let David know the outcome of this. He would communicate with David in a secretive way so that no one would be aware of it. On the third day he would come to the rock where David would be hiding and fire three arrows. If the arrows landed on the side of the rock nearest to Jonathan ("on this side of thee") then all would be well, and David would be safe to return to the palace. However, if the arrows landed on the far side of the rock and Jonathan shouted, "the arrows are beyond thee", then David must leave and leave quickly as Saul sought his life. So, after agreeing this plan and making this solemn covenant, they separate.

Sometimes we reach crunch points in life about whether to go forwards or backwards, left or right. This friendship was critical in deciding the will of God. It is important to notice that there was no talk of a plot to kill the king or a campaign of undermining him or indeed a reform agenda. Even when leadership is tragically sick, we must not resort to the world's tactics. There are some systems that have no scriptural authority at all, and the only answer is to leave them, not stay and reform them.

In the 19th century many in the UK and across the world realised that the denominations they were in had no basis in Scripture, and the hierarchies that kept the churches in check had no biblical foundation for their existence. Christians left denominations to gather to the name of the Lord Jesus alone. These were incredible decisions and full of personal pain. The resolution was so costly, and because they paid so highly for these truths, they never would sell it again cheaply (Prov 23:23). If we had asked such to stay and reform the church or take on the "Minister" directly and win the argument, they would say that with Paul that "... the weapons of our warfare are not carnal" (2 Cor 10:4), and the only thing they could do was to leave the system all together and be gathered to Christ alone. (The grave danger is that people later can go back to that very thing which their forefathers paid dearly to leave.) Many left ornate cathedrals and their elaborate rituals for a small room and kitchen with a few gathered around a loaf and cup and an open Bible. In the same way David would leave for a cave called Adullam (1 Sam 22). It was not a very exciting place, but there the people gathered to David and in a very simple but profound manner had fellowship with the Lord and one another. The challenge of this call still remains for every child of God.

The only matter that concerned David at this stage was whether he should stay or go. We can sometimes complicate our decisions by considering actions that we have no authority to execute. Also, there was no sense of what he would do if he were to go. There was a simple matter of faith that if the Lord wanted him to go then He would look after him. These decisions to leave because of fear can be terrifying. Should a family leave a community where the opposition to the gospel is endangering their lives and that of their children? Should a brother or sister leave their employment where the employer is damaging them physically and mentally? Paul deals with conundrums like this in 1 Corinthians 7. No Christian is required to remain in these dangerous situations and Scripture says that "God hath called us to peace" (1 Cor 7:15). However, each believer must weigh up such decisions before God. There may be other crunch resolutions that are not so alarming as these examples, but they are nevertheless massive in our lives. Should we move house? Should we change jobs? In all this we are simply depending upon God to look after us, knowing we do not have all the answers. The good thing to know is that the Lord will guide us if we are willing to be led: "I will instruct thee and teach thee in the way which thou shalt go: I will guide thee with mine eye" (Ps 32:8).

The feast (vv 24-34)

Jonathan arrives at the feast and on the first day Saul does not ask his son why David is not there, presuming him to have been unwell and perhaps ceremonially unclean. On the second day Saul enquires after David to Jonathan, and Jonathan replies that there was a special family meal in Bethlehem, and that David had asked his permission to be excused. (We do not believe he needed to say this, even if David had suggested it (v 6) – another example of the right thing being done in the wrong way. Unreasonable behaviour by others can make good people sin. David's plan almost caused the death of Jonathan. We do not know the implications of the smallest sin). King Saul flies into a rage when he hears this and accuses Jonathan of choosing David as the next King and grossly insults him by telling Jonathan that he is no son of his or he would not have acted in this way. We can only imagine the pain to Jonathan to be told by his father that he is illegitimate and the son of a prostitute (v 30). Saul commands Jonathan to arrest David and bring him before the king so that he can kill him. When Jonathan protests, in his anger Saul throws a javelin at him. We do not know what hurt Jonathan most - the javelin or the horrible words.

When people lose their temper and intemperate language leaves their mouth the effects can be devastating. Jonathan does not eat that night and on the morning of the third day Jonathan leaves to go the stone Ezel (meaning departure) where David is hiding to convey the sad news that he must leave and run for his life.

Jonathan thought his father would never do this (v 2), but now he knows the true character of his parent. There are moments when we are spectacularly let down by those we love. Jonathan is now realising that he is in a kingdom where God has left the king and the kingdom, and he is in a home full of hatred. What do we do in situations like this? In Jonathan's case he is determined to protect David from harm, but he does not see that God is also guiding him to leave the whole sorry system behind and be a fugitive with David. Sadly, he never took that step.

The firing of the arrows (vv 35-42)

A young boy accompanies Jonathan so as not to arouse suspicion that he is meeting David in a clandestine fashion and can verify that Jonathan was simply practicing with the bow and arrow. When they reach the appointed hour, the third day, and the appointed place, Ezel, Jonathan fires the arrow beyond the stone Ezel, three times. He then asks the young lad to run and pick up the arrows and take them back into the city, shouting after him that the arrows are "beyond thee" (v 37). The young boy does as he is told not knowing that a hidden king, David, is watching his every move and hears the message. That message is clear to David, and it is an unequivocal word – "Depart". The time has come for David to leave. After the boy has gone, David comes out of hiding and has an emotional farewell with Jonathan reiterating their love and the solemn promise to each other that they had made earlier.

In life there are moments when we must move on. It could be graduation from school, college, university. It could be the day we leave the family home or are called to go another part of the country or world. Sometimes the answer to our prayers is that, "the arrows are beyond thee". We must go! Arrows in Scripture have a variety of meanings, but one of them is divine guidance through the Scriptures. It is always a comfort when we know the Lord has told us to leave. When we see the arrows of Scripture thud into the path beyond us then, no matter how emotional the parting is and how much we miss those we leave behind, we know we are doing the right thing and the Lord will be with us. The tears are real but there would be greater tears and more sorrow if we stayed.

It is always sad when it means we must leave those behind whom we know stand for better things – but sometimes we have no choice, and for the cause of Christ we must do that which is right. If Jonathan would not come with him then David will go alone. We must honour the Lord even if good people stay back. Many have faced this when a potential life partner fails to want to honour the Lord in their life and the other realises that this "friendship" must end, or they will not be able to serve the Lord as He would want them to. Whilst not minimising the pain of parting, the decision to separate from a courtship like this is correct and the bigger disaster would be staying.

David and Jonathan embrace each other with real and genuine affection. We already knew that Jonathan loved David "as he loved his own soul" (v 17). They both realise that this is the point of parting. David's sorrow exceeds Jonathan's as he knows Jonathan is also in danger. Sadly, Jonathan returns to the house of hatred possibly thinking he will go to this dead system and try and reform it by his presence. The words chill us: "Jonathan went into the city" (v 42). Many have thought the same over the centuries and sit in dead systems of religion hoping to see it transformed. Oh, that they would hear the call of God to "Come out of her, my people" (Rev 18:4). Our convictions will always be costly and there is always a price to pay.

The boy collecting the arrows was unaware that he was communicating a very important message. How often do we hear God using children or immature Christians to direct experienced saints without knowing that they are doing this? Children ask simple questions or make simple statements of faith that can catch us by surprise: "Out of the mouth of babes and sucklings thou hast perfected praise" (Matt 21:16). It was a boy with five small loaves and two fish who brought them to the Saviour and fed 5,000 whilst older people wondered what they could do. It was a little maid that knew what Naaman should do when he caught leprosy (2 Kings 5). The arrow of Scripture can sometimes come with renewed force when carried by children.

It is interesting that all of this happens on the third day. The day of resurrection, new life, new starts. This is going to commence a new chapter in the life of David from servant of Saul to stranger; from friend of Saul to fugitive. We too must learn that our calling is to be "strangers and pilgrims" (1 Peter 2:11). We have no real home down here, and we are citizens of heaven (Phil 3:20). Like David we must go "without the camp" (Heb 13:13). The day we take this step is the day we save our spiritual lives.

Chapter 21

Running for his life

In 1 Samuel 20 David's departure is signalled by arrows, but now in 1 Samuel 21 he is running for his life. He runs initially to Nob (vv 1-9) seeking provisions where the priests were and then, sadly, he runs to Gath (vv 10-15), a Philistine town, seeking asylum.

Nob vv 1-9

Seeking provisions

David first runs to the House of God in Nob where the priest Ahimelech resided. When we are running for our life we need food, protection, and shelter. He gets food and arms from Ahimelech and later he will get shelter for a short period of time from the King of Gath. We can only understand this chapter if we understand the context of a crisis. David has made the right decision to leave the palace but that does not mean he knows what he is going to do next. We should not underestimate the stress of not knowing where shelter or food or clothing is going to be found, or how bills will be paid. David is at a cracking point, and he makes several mistakes as a result. Pray for those who are in a crisis as they are vulnerable to acting in manner that is out of character. David's transition from friend to fugitive reminds us of our transition periods. These are dangerous times, and we need forbearance with one another, support, and love. Psalm 56 and Psalm 34 were written at this time. It is in these experiences that we learn God and as a result can be used in the future to benefit others. A preacher from Scotland, John Douglas, use to say, "If David's heart had ne'er been wrung, then David's psalms had ne'er been sung". His wanderings and life hammered out on the anvil of experiences with God led to the wisdom of these psalms. They are there for all of us in transition times when we feel our vulnerability.

When David runs to the priest Ahimelech in Nob, Ahimelech is concerned and worried. Why was David alone and with no army with him? Why was Ahimelech not given advance warning? Is there a problem he should know about? David calms his fears saying he is on secret business of the King. On the one hand we should commend David that he did not spread rumours about King Saul and try to give his side of the story which is, sadly, all too often the response in conflict. "He that is first in his own cause seemeth just" (Prov 18:17)! Saul's grievous behaviour towards David would come out ultimately, but David did not want to destabilise the Kingdom any further. He certainly was on secret business, but it is a pity he said his business was on the commandment of the King, which was a lie unless he meant the Lord. Sometimes in a crisis we can tell lies. We need to be aware that this is dishonouring to the Lord. Paul writes, "Lie not one to another, seeing that ye have put off the old man with his deeds" (Col 3:9). We must believe that God will sustain us even if we cannot explain everything to everyone's satisfaction.

David asks for food for his own needs and those of the few men that were in his company (vv 3-5). He asks for five loaves, so obviously there were not too many others with him. The only food that was available was the shewbread that had been on the Golden Table in the Tabernacle for one week and was being replaced with fresh hot bread.

This bread was holy and was only for the priests to eat. Ahimelech asks if the group were ceremonially clean, that is, they had not been involved in any sexual relations with their wives. David affirms this, saying that they have been on the run for three days. The priest then permits them to eat the shewbread as they were "sanctified". The Lord used this incident when, in Matthew 12:1-9, He explained that in a humanitarian crisis the fact that they were hungry and in real need was more important than the temple protocols. This principle is still with us today. If we saw someone in a car accident just before we went to break bread with the Lord's people, then our help to those injured would take precedence over worship. There are matters which are accepted in a time of crisis that are unacceptable in normal times. The important thing is that this only happened in the crisis, and thereafter the priests alone ate the shewbread. So, we need to ensure that we do not use crisis conditions to determine what happens normally, but we must also not insist on normal conditions applying in a crisis. First and foremost, we should be marked by compassion and forbearance.

Ahimelech also gave David a sword (vv 7-9). It was the sword of Goliath. Unfortunately, David again lied saying that "the king's business required haste"! We often have to lie repeatedly after we lie once. David may have tried to justify to himself that the "king'" meant God, but David is still giving the priest the impression that it is Saul. He may have rationalised it by thinking that he did not want Ahimelech to be compromised – in the end that plan back-fired. As we have seen time and again truth always works and is blessed. If we feel we cannot say anything then best to say nothing.

David had not needed to take a sword when he defeated Goliath, just his sling, and there is something rather sad that he carries Goliath's sword now. He would be preserved without Goliath's sword, but our minds often do not think straight in a crisis, and we feel the need for protection and clutch at anything, even the world's ideas! In all of this we have one central verse that chills us – verse 7- this was all being observed by Doeg the Edomite. In the next chapter we will learn why this is so significant. This man secretly has no time for spiritual things and will use this incident as an opportunity to advance his own cause and destroy the priesthood. In times of crisis, it is possible by our behaviour that we give opportunity for carnal men to rise to prominence. The Proverbs warn us about listening to the slander of carnal men: "The words of a talebearer are as wounds, and they go down into the innermost parts of the belly" (Prov 18:8).

When Elijah was in a crisis an angel gave him food and sleep (1 Kings 19). When we see saints in a crisis we need to be like Ahimelech and give what is required and pray that they will not do anything in the emergency which they later deeply regret. If we are aware of saints struggling then we ought to help them, but also keep the matters away from carnal people and simply tell the Lord.

Gath vv 10-15

Seeking asylum

If things were bad in Nob, they now get worse. David runs to Achish the King of Gath (vv 10-15). The man that slew the Philistine runs to them for protection. When we treat God's people badly there is no saying what mistakes they will make. Of course, the Philistines see David not now as the warrior king who slew Goliath, but as a feeble fugitive seeking refuge. David realises he has made a major mistake coming here and is very afraid of Achish. He decides the only course of action is to fake a severe mental illness and he starts to crawl about on his hands and knees, scrabbling at the door like a dog and allowing his saliva to fall on his beard. The strategy seems to work and Achish commands that they throw the "mad man" out of his court, and David escapes. Sometimes God saves us despite our utter foolishness.

The lesson from this chapter surely is that when God directs us (as he did with David in chapter 19) to leave we must believe He will also direct us where to go. In our panic we can make foolish decisions, and it is only by the grace of God that these decisions do not end in disaster. This is especially true when we lack food, sleep and shelter. Can we not all look back and see how God has preserved us when we made wrong choices?

David will run now to a cave in southern Judah and there he will repent of his sins, find restoration, and be strengthened by other believers who come to him. He seeks the mind of God for what he should do next. He is at his safest in the cave of Adullam. Often the lesson in a crisis is that our "... strength is to sit still" (Isa 30:7).

Between chapter 21 and chapter 22 the learning of Psalm 34 is brought before us. David comes out of this a much wiser man and would never forget the preservation he experienced from the Lord.

PSALM 56

[To the chief Musician upon Jonathelemrechokim, Michtam
of David, when the Philistines took him in Gath.]

¹ Be merciful unto me, O God: for man would swallow me up; he fighting daily oppresseth me.

² Mine enemies would daily swallow me up: for they be many that fight against me, O thou most High.

³ What time I am afraid, I will trust in thee.

⁴ In God I will praise his word, in God I have put my trust; I will not fear what flesh can do unto me.

⁵ Every day they wrest my words: all their thoughts are against me for evil.

⁶ They gather themselves together, they hide themselves, they mark my steps, when they wait for my soul.

⁷ Shall they escape by iniquity? in thine anger cast down the people, O God.

⁸ Thou tellest my wanderings: put thou my tears into thy bottle: are they not in thy book?

⁹ When I cry unto thee, then shall mine enemies turn back: this I know; for God is for me.

¹⁰ In God will I praise his word: in the LORD will I praise his word.

¹¹ In God have I put my trust: I will not be afraid what man can do unto me.

12 Thy vows are upon me, O God: I will render praises unto thee.

13 For thou hast delivered my soul from death: wilt not thou deliver my feet from falling, that I may walk before God in the light of the living?

PSALM 34

[A Psalm of David, when he changed his behaviour before Abimelech; who drove him away, and he departed.]

[1] I will bless the LORD at all times: his praise shall continually be in my mouth.

[2] My soul shall make her boast in the LORD: the humble shall hear thereof, and be glad.

[3] O magnify the LORD with me, and let us exalt his name together.

[4] I sought the LORD, and he heard me, and delivered me from all my fears.

[5] They looked unto him, and were lightened: and their faces were not ashamed.

[6] This poor man cried, and the LORD heard him, and saved him out of all his troubles.

[7] The angel of the LORD encampeth round about them that fear him, and delivereth them.

[8] O taste and see that the LORD is good: blessed is the man that trusteth in him.

⁹ O fear the LORD, ye his saints: for there is no want to them that fear him.

¹⁰ The young lions do lack, and suffer hunger: but they that seek the LORD shall not want any good thing.

¹¹ Come, ye children, hearken unto me: I will teach you the fear of the LORD.

¹² What man is he that desireth life, and loveth many days, that he may see good?

¹³ Keep thy tongue from evil, and thy lips from speaking guile.

¹⁴ Depart from evil, and do good; seek peace, and pursue it.

¹⁵ The eyes of the LORD are upon the righteous, and his ears are open unto their cry.

¹⁶ The face of the LORD is against them that do evil, to cut off the remembrance of them from the earth.

¹⁷ The righteous cry, and the LORD heareth, and delivereth them out of all their troubles.

¹⁸ The LORD is nigh unto them that are of a broken heart; and saveth such as be of a contrite spirit.

¹⁹ Many are the afflictions of the righteous: but the LORD delivereth him out of them all.

²⁰ He keepeth all his bones: not one of them is broken.

²¹ Evil shall slay the wicked: and they that hate the righteous shall be desolate.

²² The LORD redeemeth the soul of his servants: and none of them that trust in him shall be desolate.

CHAPTER 6

David: His Cave

1 Samuel 22

David escapes from the King of Gath and runs to the cave of Adullam in southern Judah, and in his isolation, he proved God. This next set of chapters (Chs 22-26) show the fellowship David enjoyed as a fugitive in the cave of Adullam, the hold, the forest of Hareth, Keilah and the wilderness of Ziph. They confirm that fellowship can grow even in adversity and God guides us when we seek him in every aspect of our lives, even in days of trauma.

For David, isolation meant greater fellowship with God and His people in the cave of Adullam (1 Sam 22). In Keilah, isolation meant even greater dependency upon God for guidance (1 Sam 23). In Engedi and Carmel, isolation taught David lessons of patience in restraint (1 Sam 24-26).

Fellowship in the cave of Adullam

David moves out alone, sure that God has told him to leave the palace and goes from Nob to Gath and on to a large limestone cave in the wilderness of southern Judah, called Adullam, about 12 miles south-west of Bethlehem. Psalm 57 and Psalm 142 were written there. It is here that he learns God in a way that he never knew Him before and would never forget. In his isolation he was being prepared for reigning. It was also here that he learned the true meaning of fellowship as many others joined him. God sometimes gives us a work to do in a crisis that we could not have foreseen, and people emerge who we did not know and seek fellowship with us in the outside place. There are seven principles of fellowship in this chapter.

Fellowship is gathering together with a rejected King, away from the world

Four hundred people come to the cave of Adullam to be with David (v 2) and this grows to six hundred in the next chapter (23:13)! This increase in followers reminds us of Gideon who was alone threshing wheat in a winepress to hide it from the Midianites before being joined a few days later by 32,000 people (Judges 6-7). Being alone with God can result in greater fellowship with God and His people. David takes the outside place and people are drawn to him. It says in verse 1 that "they went ... to him", and in verse 2 that they "gathered themselves unto him". In Adullam the attraction was David. David was the circumference and centre of their fellowship.

The cave of Adullam is a lovely picture of the Assembly of God's people. We also gather in the outside place to a rejected King, the Lord Jesus Christ, alone. He is the attraction. We remove ourselves from all ecclesiastical systems and gather "outside the camp" to the Lord Jesus, taking no other name or authority: "Let us go forth therefore **unto him** without the camp, bearing his reproach. For here have we no continuing city, but we seek one to come" (Heb 13:13-14). All sectarian titles are unscriptural. Just as they gathered "unto David", so Christ is the magnet and the mandate for our gatherings. He created "the fellowship" not us. It was not the salubrious surroundings that drew David's disciples but the rejected King. So, with God's people today the attraction to gather together is not in the architecture, or the music, or even the enthusiastic preaching, but to be with our blessed Saviour, the Lord Jesus Christ who promises to be "in the midst" (Matt 18:20): "To whom coming, as unto a living stone, disallowed indeed of men, but chosen of God, and precious" (1 Pet 2:4).

David's followers would not be in the cave all day; they would be out scouting the area, gathering food etc. Let us remember that those in fellowship in an Assembly of God's people are still gathered unto the Lord Jesus even if we are not gathered together physically. David became their captain (v 2) and surely our Chief and Head is Christ. We are answerable to Him. What authority! What liberty!

Fellowship can result in an unexpected and unusual set of people coming together

We read in verse 1 that his brothers and family join him: "and when his brethren and all his father's house heard it, they went down thither to him". This was the same family that did not think he would ever be King; the same brothers who belittled him in saying, "with whom hast thou left those few sheep in the wilderness?" (1 Sam 17:28). Perhaps the crisis has made them re-evaluate matters. They had seen Samuel anoint David King and now they acknowledge that David is indeed the King. Sometimes crises can do this – convictions can form when people are forced to make a choice. These brothers now leave the paid army of King Saul and endanger their lives by becoming fugitives with David. They had not believed when Samuel anointed him in Bethlehem in front of them all (1 Sam 16), but now they believe and come and join David in a day of rejection. This unexpected development encourages us to keep praying for loved ones. Sometimes in a crisis people who have not made the spiritual progress that the Lord would have for them, come to see this great truth of gathering alone to the Lord Jesus.

But who else came to David? Those distressed, those in debt and discontented: "And every one that was in distress, and every one that was in debt, and every one that was discontented, gathered themselves unto him; and he became a captain over them: and there were with him about four hundred men" (23:2). What a motley crew! When God saves us from our sins and brings us into His House, it is not that we are anything special. Far from it! Paul says of the Corinthian assembly: "Know ye not that the unrighteous shall not inherit the kingdom of God? Be not deceived: neither fornicators, nor idolaters, nor adulterers, nor effeminate, nor abusers of themselves with mankind, Nor thieves, nor covetous, nor drunkards, nor revilers, nor extortioners, shall inherit the kingdom of God. And such were some of you: but ye are washed, but ye are sanctified, but ye are justified in the name of the Lord Jesus, and by the Spirit of our God" (1 Cor 6:9-11). It is the Lord Jesus that fits us to be in His presence.

Therefore, the thing that is attractive about the Assembly is the Lord Jesus Christ and not the people. We have nothing to be proud about – we are simply sinners saved by grace. The character of the Corinthians before they were saved was appalling. However, the changed lives of the Corinthians were a demonstration of the power of Christ: "And such were some of you: but ...". The people who came to David in Adullam were changed. David became a captain to them and shaped them into an incredible army. There was not another David, just as there is only one Lord Jesus Christ. The person we are drawn to is Christ and He will shape us and help us to love our brothers and sisters (1 John 5:1). First and foremost, the fellowship we have is with the Father and with His son Jesus Christ and following from this comes our horizontal fellowship with one another. The Lord Jesus said: "By this shall all men know that ye are my disciples, if ye have love one to another" (John 13:35).

The fellowship in Adullam would have been strengthened by the fact that outside the cave there was danger to everyone and inside the cave was safety. On every head was a price. Saul wanted to slay them all. Each looked out for one another's safety. True fellowship is realising the world around us is polluted and vile and we have in each other true friendship and support and purpose to serve the Lord. This is what makes fellowship so special. When we are alone, we can be occupied with our problems, but in the fellowship we learn that some have far greater problems than we do - for example, the Abiathar mentioned later in the chapter lost all of his family, executed on Saul's orders for daring to give David provisions! This interest in others helps us from being preoccupied with self. Serving others is a great antidote to sadness (Phil 2:4).

Fellowship will result in acts of self-sacrifice and devotion for the Lord and His people

Also, within the fellowship some of the greatest examples of self-sacrifice take place. It was here, in the cave of Adullam, that three of the company broke through the ranks of the Philistines to get to a well in Bethlehem because David had simply wished for a drink of water! David was so touched by this he poured it out before the Lord (2 Sam

23:13-17). Some of the greatest examples of sacrifice and devotion to the Lord happen when we appreciate the person of Christ and the fellowship we have been brought into. Paul encouraged the Galatian assemblies: "Bear ye one another's burdens, and so fulfil the law of Christ" (Gal 6:2). Separation to the Lord encourages us all to see that we have no greater purpose to live for than serving the Lord and His people.

Fellowship includes making provision for the vulnerable

Sometimes the fellowship is not complete. There are people who should be there who are not. In David case this was his mother and father (vv 3-5). During this time David made provision for his parents in the land of Moab. In one respect he was foreshadowing the Lord Jesus. The Lord looked after his mother at the cross, inviting John to care for her, as her son (John 19:26-27). David certainly believed in honouring his father and mother and did not want them to be pursued by Saul, perhaps thinking that the cave was not conducive to their health. We must look after those most vulnerable in our company. This became a major feature of the early church as they looked after the genuine widows in the assembly (compare 1 Timothy 5 or the early verses of Acts 6).

This is a principle we can learn from David, who asks the King of Moab to look after his parents, after all his great-grandmother had been a Moabite (Ruth 4). This might just picture a truth found much later in our Bible. It is clear from Isaiah 16 that in the future when Israel is being attacked, and the millions of troops gather at Armageddon for the final battle, God's people will in their terror escape into Moab (present day Jordan) for refuge. Some individuals in Moab will protect them from the carnage: "Let mine outcasts dwell with thee, Moab; be thou a covert to them from the face of the spoiler: for the extortioner is at an end, the spoiler ceaseth, the oppressors are consumed out of the land" (Isa 16:4). It is perhaps for this reason that they seem to be protected when the Man of Sin enters the land (Dan 11:41): "He shall enter also into the glorious land, and many countries shall be overthrown: but these shall escape out of his hand, even Edom, and Moab, and the chief of the children of Ammon". So, David's action with his parents may be mirroring a great prophetic truth for the nation as well.

However, whilst we can see these important principles and prophetic pictures, we are still not sure how wise David was in this decision. Moab was a traditional enemy of Israel with idolatrous practices (Deut 23:2-6), and David did not appear to ask for guidance before settling his parents there. Is it ever right to go to Moab? Moab is a picture of the flesh. Big King Eglon sitting gorging in his summerhouse seems to represent their character (Judges 3:15-30). The Scriptures state: "We have heard the pride of Moab, (he is exceeding proud) his loftiness, and his arrogancy, and his pride, and the haughtiness of his heart" (Jer 48:29). A proud, self-sufficient, worldly lifestyle is the description by Jeremiah: "Moab has been at ease from his youth, and he hath settled on his lees" (Jer 48:11). This expression "settled on his lees" refers to the sediment at the bottom of a bottle. Moab is wealthy, never having known what it is to be turned upside down, simply resting on all he has and unconcerned about others. We feel sure that if Ruth had been alive, she would have warned David about going down to Moab and reminded him of Orpah who never came back (Ruth 1). We are also not sure how well the Moabites treated David's parents before they returned to him. Judging by the ruthless way David later dealt with Moab it is possible that his parents were not well treated (2 Sam 8:2). Sometimes in a crisis we make wrong decisions. We can understand David's logic: the older couple would be vulnerable, and they could have been a burden to others. Let us be on our guard. David and his parents missed fellowship with each other when he was in Adullam.

We do not have Scripture for sending vulnerable people away from the fellowship because a different place we feel would suit them better. People have done this with their children, for example, and kept them away from the Assembly gatherings, often with their academic interest at heart – but this is disaster. Remember, Moab is associated with idleness. There are places where we can settle down to do nothing very much for the Lord and neglect the fellowship of God's people. The Hebrew writer warns: "And let us consider one another to provoke unto love and to good works: Not forsaking the assembling of ourselves together, as the manner of some is; but exhorting one another: and so much the more, as ye see the day approaching" (Heb 10:24-25).

Our duty, therefore, is to look after the vulnerable in the assembly and not send them away. How do we look out for them? We must always remember that these are our brothers and sisters for whom Christ died. The Scriptures are clear about our responsibilities to widows and the homeless: "Pure religion and undefiled before God is this, To visit the fatherless and widows in their affliction" (James 1:27). May God help us to rise to our responsibilities in the fellowship.

Fellowship is not built on fear or guilt, but love

David moves from the hold to the forest of Hareth on the prophet Gad's counsel. Gad is called David's seer (1 Chron 21.9) and would be with him right to the end, writing a book about David's reign (1 Chron 29:29) and encouraging him in the song of worship in the sanctuary (2 Chron 29:25). It is when David and all his men are in the forest of Hareth that we learn the dreadful story of Doeg the Edomite killing the priests in Nob. Doeg tells Saul that David had been to the priest and eaten the shewbread and taken Goliath's sword, implying that the priest Ahimlech is in a conspiracy with David against Saul.

It is here in Ramah that we see a picture of carnal leadership in Saul and a carnal congregation. It is not the cave of Adullam but a conference under a tree in Ramah, near Gibeah, where King Saul presides (v 6): "When Saul heard that David was discovered, and the men that were with him, (now Saul abode in Gibeah under a tree in Ramah, having his spear in his hand, and all his servants were standing about him)". Saul is asking questions about loyalty to him. The spear in his hand reminds us that his leadership style keeps people together by fear. People are afraid to let him down, and, in order to show that they are not loyal to David, carry out acts they would otherwise never do. It stands in contrast to the leadership of David in Adullam where affection for David led to people serving him. When he was the captain of Saul's army, David had trained officers, and people would jump to do his bidding, but things were different now. The fellowship of David was bound together and motivated by love. David fashioned this group into a fighting force. He had been used to a disciplined, trained army with full compliance and respect, but now he makes ordinary people something they could never have achieved alone. What a contrast between the two groups!

In the carnal congregation Saul tries to make people feel sorry for him (v 8): "That all of you have conspired against me, and there is none that sheweth me that my son hath made a league with the son of Jesse, and there is none of you that is sorry for me, or sheweth unto me that my son hath stirred up my servant against me, to lie in wait, as at this day?". We see these same false characteristics of leadership in the world today. People make others feel sorry for them and then make demands of them. The system is driven by fear and guilt. Again, this is such a contrast to Adullam, where people serve David and his followers out of love, not out of a sense of guilt or pity. In the Assembly today it is the same principle. Paul reminds the Ephesians: "Be ye therefore followers of God, as dear children; And walk in love, as Christ also hath loved us, and hath given himself for us an offering and a sacrifice to God for a sweet-smelling savour" (Eph 5:1-2).

Fellowship and priesthood are intricately linked

In the carnal congregation Edomites have been given power over priests. Doeg is permitted to slander and accuse priestly men of plotting against the King (vv 9-11). There is no evidence, for example, that Ahimilech did enquire with the Urim and the Thummim for David, but no serious exploration of the facts is carried out by Saul, instead there is a rushed and tragic judgment of death for the priests (vv 12-16). We need to watch whose advice we heed, and we should not allow good people to be maligned. It is possible for us to see this today; worldly men could be given place among God's people, and then destroy those that are spiritual. Through asserting control, everyone else is afraid to say anything. It is a fellowship of fear. The carnal mind is at enmity with God. Ahimelech's simple answer of innocence that he was unaware that David was going against the King, and that he did not know of any fracture in the relationship between Saul and David is swept aside. Truth is not important but sending a message of fear and compliance to the nation is.

In the end, Doeg the Edomite destroys Nob including the animals and sucklings (v 19). He has no heart at all. Eighty-five priests are slain. We must not think that the worldly man is neutral to spiritual subjects such as priesthood. Priesthood allows us to draw near to God. It is a beautiful truth enjoyed by all believers, but many have missed this truth and prevent the people of God serving as part of a priesthood in the House of God: "To whom coming, as unto a living stone ... Ye also, as lively stones, are built up a spiritual house, an holy priesthood, to offer up spiritual sacrifices, acceptable to God by Jesus Christ" (1 Peter2:4-5). A system of clerisy has been devised that has decimated the priesthood principle – in this system only a special few can draw near to God or speak for God. This system cannot alter the fact that our fellowship with the Lord Jesus in God's House starts and ends with priestly activity. The work of Doeg the Edomite is still active and like Abiathar the priest in this chapter, each exercised priest must leave places that dishonour this principle and run to the place of the rejected King, an Assembly of believers linked solely to the Name of the Lord Jesus. It is there they can function as a priesthood in the fellowship of God's House. We must never treat these things casually, and need to be on our guard against anything that seeks to gnaw away at the truth of the priestly practices of the assembly.

Fellowship can expand in a time of crisis

The ugliness of this whole scene results in a priest, Abiathar, running to be with David (v 20). There he finds a place where priesthood is treasured: "And one of the sons of Ahimelech the son of Ahitub, named Abiathar, escaped, and fled after David". Sometimes the greatest of expansions of the fellowship have been in the most trying of circumstances. Days of isolation or rejection can prove to be the days when people come to see that true fellowship is simple, and being faithful to the Lord is all that matters.

It is lovely to see how David received Abiathar: "Abide thou with me, fear not: for he that seeketh my life seeketh thy life: but with me thou shalt be in safeguard" (v 23). When people join an Assembly of God's people, however, they must be assured of acceptance and love. Abiathar also comes ready to serve as a priest with the ephod in his hand: "And it came to pass, when Abiathar the son of Ahimelech fled to David to Keilah, that he came down with an ephod in his hand" (23:6). When people join an Assembly, they must realise they are contributing to the fellowship as a priest and that they have an important role to play.

David has the prophet Gad with him, and now he has the priest Abiathar, and David is the rightful King. Sometimes in times of dreadful sin there can come tokens of blessing and encouragement to the faithful. The fellowship is expanding but in dreadful circumstances. God often blesses in adversity and a time of loss. There are, therefore, simple principles of fellowship for us to learn during David's stay in the cave of Adullam.

PSALM 57

[To the chief Musician, Altaschith, Michtam of David, when he fled from Saul in the cave.]

¹ Be merciful unto me, O God, be merciful unto me: for my soul trusteth in thee: yea, in the shadow of thy wings will I make my refuge, until these calamities be overpast.

² I will cry unto God most high; unto God that performeth all things for me.

³ He shall send from heaven, and save me from the reproach of him that would swallow me up. Selah. God shall send forth his mercy and his truth.

⁴ My soul is among lions: and I lie even among them that are set on fire, even the sons of men, whose teeth are spears and arrows, and their tongue a sharp sword.

⁵ Be thou exalted, O God, above the heavens; let thy glory be above all the earth.

⁶ They have prepared a net for my steps; my soul is bowed down: they have digged a pit before me, into the midst whereof they are fallen themselves. Selah.

⁷ My heart is fixed, O God, my heart is fixed: I will sing and give praise.

⁸ Awake up, my glory; awake, psaltery and harp: I myself will awake early.

⁹ I will praise thee, O Lord, among the people: I will sing unto thee among the nations.

¹⁰ For thy mercy is great unto the heavens, and thy truth unto the clouds

¹¹ Be thou exalted, O God, above the heavens: let thy glory be above all the earth.

PSALM 142

[Maschil of David; A Prayer when he was in the cave]

¹ I cried unto the LORD with my voice; with my voice unto the LORD did I make my supplication.

² I poured out my complaint before him; I shewed before him my trouble.

³ When my spirit was overwhelmed within me, then thou knewest my path. In the way wherein I walked have they privily laid a snare for me.

⁴ I looked on my right hand, and beheld, but there was no man that would know me: refuge failed me; no man cared for my soul.

⁵ I cried unto thee, O LORD: I said, Thou art my refuge and my portion in the land of the living.

⁶ Attend unto my cry; for I am brought very low: deliver me from my persecutors; for they are stronger than I.

⁷ Bring my soul out of prison, that I may praise thy name: the righteous shall compass me about; for thou shalt deal bountifully with me.

PSALM 52

[To the chief Musician, Maschil, A Psalm of David, when Doeg the Edomite came and told Saul, and said unto him, David is come to the house of Ahimelech.]

[1] Why boastest thou thyself in mischief, O mighty man? the goodness of God endureth continually.

[2] Thy tongue deviseth mischiefs; like a sharp razor, working deceitfully.

[3] Thou lovest evil more than good; and lying rather than to speak righteousness. Selah.

[4] Thou lovest all devouring words, O thou deceitful tongue.

[5] God shall likewise destroy thee for ever, he shall take thee away, and pluck thee out of thy dwelling place, and root thee out of the land of the living. Selah.

[6] The righteous also shall see, and fear, and shall laugh at him:

[7] Lo, this is the man that made not God his strength; but trusted in the abundance of his riches, and strengthened himself in his wickedness.

[8] But I am like a green olive tree in the house of God: I trust in the mercy of God for ever and ever.

[9] I will praise thee for ever, because thou hast done it: and I will wait on thy name; for it is good before thy saints.

CHAPTER 7

David: His Counsel

1 Samuel 23

This chapter teaches us lessons about David's intercession in times of persecution and God's counsel and guidance in his life. God instructs David to go and save the town of Keilah from the marauding forces of the Philistines, and then directs him to leave.

God will guide us if we ask and are exercised to know His will

The biggest lesson in life is simple dependency upon the Lord. The Philistines were robbing the threshing floors of the town of Keilah. David was stationed close by, only three miles south of Adullam in the fertile Judean plains. This is a classic Philistine tactic: starving the people of God. In Genesis they filled the wells of refreshment with earth so that there would be no water (Gen 26:15). When God's people are forced to isolate or find themselves in a crisis by carnal influence, then often a famine commences, not necessarily of physical food but of hearing the "words of the LORD" (Amos 8:11).

David learned how to trust God for guidance on all his movements: "Therefore, David enquired of the LORD, saying, Shall I go and smite these Philistines?" (v 2). He had previously listened to the voice of God via the prophet Gad and now he is seeking the mind of God via the priest Abiathar. It is good to know that God has promised to guide His people if we ask: "I will instruct thee and teach thee in the way which thou shalt go: I will guide thee with mine eye" (Ps 32:8). We have the Holy Spirit, and the Saviour said of Him: "Howbeit when he, the Spirit of truth, is come, he will guide you into all truth: for he shall not speak of himself; but whatsoever he shall hear, that shall he speak: and he will shew you things to come" (John 16:13). It is this guiding of the Holy Spirit that Paul relied upon in his movements (Acts 16:6-10). He will guide us today - if we ask.

God will test why we ask

God will always test our motives for requesting guidance. David asked if he should go to Keilah or not? We all should ask for direction in our lives. James warns about making moves without seeking God's guidance (James 4.13-17). David's motive for asking is also clearly stated - should he go and defeat the Philistines who were starving God's people (v 2)? As a result, the Spirit of God tells him to go and smite the Philistines: "And the LORD said unto David, Go, and smite the Philistines, and save Keilah". As with Goliath (1 Sam 17), David's motive was to destroy an enemy intent on destroying God's people, not to see some drama in the valley as his brother Eliab had once implied. David's desire was solely for the honour of God.

It is good when we are clear in our mind what the Lord is telling us to do and why we are asking to do it. We do not always get such a clear response, but we should expect God to guide us, and, in His time, He will make it clear to us if our motive is pure. In this case David was not doing it out of convenience, or because it suited him. This is not prayer to God asking for some luxury. There is no sense of self-indulgence here. It is all for the glory of God.

When the following three things align it is normally a good indication of God's will for us:

1. An initial desire and exercise of soul which has a true motive

2. Clear Scripture for doing what we are exercised to do

3. Circumstances coming together to make a course of action possible without it being contrived or orchestrated.

When our motive is pure for asking for guidance the Lord Jesus tells us we should expect to be guided by God: "If any man will do his will, he shall know of the doctrine ..." (John 7:17).

God will test how we ask

David's men are afraid and question the wisdom of this action: "And David's men said unto him, Behold, we be afraid here in Judah: how much more then if we come to Keilah against the armies of the Philistines?" (23:3). We need wisdom and resilience to carry out His will, especially when it involves others. It is one thing to get clear guidance what we should do; it is quite another thing to take our brothers and sisters with us.

The fear issue is not confined to David's era - it affects all generations. David needed much wisdom as his men were afraid: if he told the people he was going anyway that would ruin the relationships he had with them and would be lacking in love; on the other hand, if he decided not to do anything until everyone felt happy then that would be wrong as God had told him to go to Keilah. The answer to this dilemma is found in the fourth verse: "Then David enquired of the LORD yet again". God is testing David's resilience, dependency, and wisdom. The answer is prayer.

Prayer changes things, including our attitude towards our brethren. Maybe on his knees David better understood his brethren's fears and need of courage. We can almost see him wrestling with God. He may have argued with himself, that this was Saul's job as King to protect his people; did he, David, need to get involved or put his men in danger? But God's people were starving in Keilah. David did not need to ask: "And who is my neighbour?" (Luke 10:29). These were God's people, and he would defend them from the Philistines. It was the right thing to do. Once again, he is directed to go with this promise that the Philistines will be given into his hand: "And the LORD answered him and said, Arise, go down to Keilah; for I will deliver the Philistines into thine hand" (v 4).

God still directs us today. He will check our motives, courage and love for our brothers and sisters and, sometimes, he sends us with a promise: "I will deliver". God challenges our resilience and our willingness to take His people with us and yet still do the right thing. God assures us that he will not only direct us but give us the enabling strength to do it, even if it is unpopular. We are not surprised then when we read the beginning of verse 5: "So David and his men went to Keilah". Nor are we surprised when we read the end of verse 5: "So David saved the inhabitants of Keilah". What else could be the outcome with such clear guidance?

Perhaps it was instances like this that made David write: "The LORD is my light and my salvation; whom shall I fear? the LORD is the strength of my life; of whom shall I be afraid?" (Ps 27:1). What do we do when God's people are afraid? We must not get angry and carry on regardless, or on the other hand do nothing. We must acknowledge the very real fears of our brothers and sisters and once again consult the Lord. However, when it is clear what the Lord is requesting, we must seek to do what is right. As believers we must do that which is right, and in love seek to carry our brethren with us. The corollary is also true; the flock should follow wise leadership and trust the decisions of local elders.

God will test if we ask again when circumstances change

David saved the inhabitants of Keilah but Saul regards David as vulnerable, being contained in a walled city. Astonishingly, Saul views this as evidence of the will of God to go and kill David: "And Saul said, God hath delivered him into mine hand; for he is shut in, by entering into a town that hath gates and bars" (v 7). We need to be very careful about using God's Name to endorse our evil objectives. The carnal man thinks circumstances only dictate God's will.

However, the fact that Saul is advancing towards David (v 8) leads David to enquire yet again of the Lord whether he should leave Keilah (vv 9-11). Guidance for doing something today does not mean it is guidance for tomorrow. We constantly need to be before God. Sometimes we must stop doing something even when it has been an activity that has been blessed in the past. God expects us to seek his guidance to go to a place, and to leave a place. James says: "For that ye ought to say, If the Lord will, we shall live, and do this, or that" (James 4:15). We need to be sensitive to the guidance of God in our lives.

God will test the assumptions we have about what we are asking

David once again enquires whether the men of Keilah would deliver him to Saul and will Saul come down? He is very specific in his request: "Will the men of Keilah deliver me up into his hand? Will Saul come down, as thy servant hath heard? O LORD God of Israel, I beseech thee, tell thy servant. And the LORD said, He will come down. Then said David, Will the men of Keilah deliver me and my men into the hand of Saul? And the LORD said, they will deliver thee up" (23:11-12).

Interestingly, in the narrative Saul never came (v 13) and the men of Keilah never gave David up because he fled. There is a most intriguing theological point here about foreknowledge. God not only knows the actual future, but He also knows what the future will be unless certain steps are taken. He knows the intentions of the human heart. That is the sort of God we have! So now David moves to the wilderness of Ziph (vv 13-14).

David may have thought that he did not need to ask about the men of Keilah as he saved them, so in turn they would look after him. But if he had made this assumption in prayer, he would have been wrong. Perhaps Keilah baulked at feeding David's army. They wanted to be liberated and then to be free to carry on with their lifestyle. In this respect Keilah is a picture of the world. No matter how much kindness we have shown to those in the world we cannot assume we will always get kindness back - remember they are the enemies of the cross of Christ. (Gal 6:14). Therefore, James says, "friendship with the world is enmity with God" (James 4:4). We need wisdom to know what God would have us do every day and not assume that guidance yesterday will do for today. God will guide us about approaching threats and show us the way of escape. God will also guide us about the world. We should expect nothing from the world - remember the Lord's words: "But love ye your enemies, and do good, and lend, hoping for nothing again; and your reward shall be great, and ye shall be the children of the Highest: for he is kind unto the unthankful and to the evil" (Luke 6:35).

But expansion can still take place even if David is not in a walled city. In fact, in verse 13 we learn that David's army increases to 600, from the 400 men in the previous chapter. Loving the world will not lead to enlargement; our expansion is contingent on our separation. Maintaining holy conditions attracts the spiritual. So let us be careful about our assumptions in prayer.

God will test our obedience as He guides us

David is found in a wood hiding from King Saul. Jonathan finds David and strengthens his hand in God: "And Jonathan Saul's son arose, and went to David into the wood, and strengthened his hand in God" (23:16). This expresses the importance of believers who visit us and help us. Sometimes, we get encouragement from the most unlikely of people at the most of unlikely of times. God leads people to come to us and encourage us – Jonathan risked his life to come and strengthen David's hand in God. This came just at exactly the right time. We too need guidance in all our movements; including whom we visit and when. Sometimes the Lord puts it into our hearts to visit others in a day of extremity. Jonathan saw in David that he was the rightful successor, "thou shalt be king" (v 17), but sadly he never left and came to be with David. He expected that would be "next unto" David saying, " ... and I shall be next unto thee" (v 17). He assumed he could turn the corrupt system he was in towards David, but, in fact, he would die with his father in Mount Gilboa in a few years' time. God will not give us any further revelation until we act on what we know. Jonathan in some way reflects those who stay in systems which they aware are unscriptural in the hope that they can serve God. The truth is God wanted Jonathan to be with David and back up his words with actions. There are multitudes of Christians in this perspective. We should pray for all such. But David is not acrimonious, nor does he criticise Jonathan – only God could reveal to him to leave the palace. David loved Jonathan – "I am distressed for thee my brother Jonathan" (2 Sam 1:26), and Jonathan had really encouraged David at a critical time. Nevertheless, Jonathan's actions tragically resulted in his service coming to a premature end. But David appreciated what Jonathan did for him. God still guides and supports us through His people, especially in days of adversity

God will test our faith as He guides us

God often takes us to the point where human explanation or resources are impossible. David is taken to this place at the end of the chapter (vv 19-29). The Ziphites secretly tell Saul that they know exactly where David is hiding and that they are prepared to deliver him up into his hands (vv 19-20). They do not seem to have any personal animosity to David – this, like Pontius Pilate later, was a political decision. They felt their future was more secure under Saul.

This attitude of the Ziphites pleases Saul well, and he asks them to identify exactly David's location. Saul then approaches with an army to arrest David (vv 21-24). David hears of this and flees into the wilderness of Maon until he is cornered by a pincer movement of Saul's forces on a mountain (vv 25-26). There is no human resource to save him: this is the moment of capture. And then, just at the point of arrest, a messenger comes to King Saul to tell that the Philistines had invaded the land, forcing Saul to leave rapidly to protect his people (vv 27-28). God in His mercy had saved and protected David. David leaves to live in Engedi.

God tests our faith. He sometimes tests us on how willing we are to be guided and dependent upon Him. David is cornered and has no way out. He is trapped - but the Lord steps in. A simple incursion of the Philistines removes King Saul from threatening David (v 27). A bad night's sleep for King Ahasuerus saves Mordecai from the gallows and puts wicked Haman there (Esther, chapters 5-7). A tear trickling down the cheek of a baby Moses turned the wheel of history and resulted in Moses' mother being paid to look after her own child on the order of Pharaoh's daughter (Ex 2:5-10). Peter was about to be killed by Herod, until an angel opened the door of the cell (Acts 12). Paul proved from experience in that in our trials God always provides "a way to escape" (1 Cor 10:13).

David would be taught that God is in control and that he could depend upon Him even when the Ziphities were plotting against him and when, humanly speaking, there seemed no way out. God can turn around all our adverse circumstances in an instant, no matter how hopeless we feel our circumstances are. We are in His hands. And our God is able to do "exceeding abundantly above all that we ask or think" (Eph 3:20).

Looking back at David's time in Keilah, in the wood and wilderness of Ziph, we learn principles about the guidance of God in our life. It is likely that it was here in the wilderness of Ziph that Psalm 54 was written.

PSALM 54

[To the chief Musician on Neginoth, Maschil, A Psalm of David, when the Ziphims came and said to Saul, Doth not David hide himself with us?]

¹ Save me, O God, by thy name, and judge me by thy strength.

² Hear my prayer, O God; give ear to the words of my mouth.

³ For strangers are risen up against me, and oppressors seek after my soul: they have not set God before them. Selah.

⁴ Behold, God is mine helper: the Lord is with them that uphold my soul.

⁵ He shall reward evil unto mine enemies: cut them off in thy truth.

⁶ I will freely sacrifice unto thee: I will praise thy name, O LORD; for it is good.

⁷ For he hath delivered me out of all trouble: and mine eye hath seen his desire upon mine enemies.

CHAPTER 8

David: His Control

1 Samuel 24-26

In Chapters 24-26 David spares Saul twice from death, and Nabal
the Carmelite from the sword, through the instrumentality of Abigail.
The chapters remind us of the need for meekness and patience to wait
for God's will to come to fruition. James says that this is something we
all must learn: "My brethren, count it all joy when ye fall into divers
temptations; Knowing this, that the trying of your faith worketh
patience. But let patience have her perfect work, that ye may be
perfect and entire, wanting nothing" (James 1:2-4).

Self-control

On two occasions in chapters 24-26, David was given opportunity to
kill Saul, but chose to spare him (ch. 24 and ch. 26). The first time, Saul
came into the cave alone where David and his men were hiding, and the
second time, David crept into Saul's camp at night and found Saul sleeping
without anybody guarding him. In both cases David passed the test of
self-control. The second test is often harder than the first. The fact that
David had to be re-tested on the same issue in chapter 26 was because he
had not fully grasped the lesson in chapter 24. Sandwiched between the
accounts in chapters 24 and 26 of David restraining himself from killing
Saul is the story of David himself being restrained from killing Nabal the
Carmelite through the instrumentality of Abigail (ch. 25). This illustrates
the Lord Jesus' teaching that the sheathed sword is more powerful than
the drawn sword (Luke 22:38; 49-51). These chapters remind us that it is
essential to have patience for God's will to come to fruition and not seek
to accelerate divine purpose. Sometimes we, too, need fellow Christians
that can help us when we act out of character.

David waited on God's timing for him to be King. The Scriptures are full of people seeking to hasten God's purpose for them. Jacob sought the blessing from Isaac by masquerading as Esau (Gen 27). We recall that Hazael, after he had heard from Elisha that he would be king of Syria, smothered his master Behadad with a sponge (2 Kings 8:7-15) to hasten the start of his reign as king. David had to learn that even when circumstances give the impression that our enemy has been delivered into our hands, we must resist the temptation from within or pressure from without to take the initiative to scheme and plot to remove the threat. As Jacob with Laban (Gen 30-31), we need patience to believe that God will vindicate us when people threaten us prejudicially.

The strip of cloth at Engedi (Chapter 24)

In chapter 24, Saul comes once again after David (v 2). This time David is found in Engedi (v 1) a rocky, desolate area of southern Judah. Amazingly Saul comes into the very cave where David and his men are found (v 3). It must have been a huge cavern to be able to hold so many people. Saul seems to be answering a call of nature, unaware that he is surrounded. David's men see an opportunity for David to kill Saul: in fact, they think that this is an opportunity sent from God (v 4). We ought to be careful how we invoke God's name to support our selfish acts. Saul had made this grave mistake using circumstances as his evidence that it was the will of God to kill David (23:7). Some of David's men have the same thinking. The will of God will never involve us doing something that is contrary to Scripture. Six hundred men watched from the inner darkness as Saul lay sleeping or preoccupied in the light at the front of the cave. One man stood between David and the whole Kingdom. Here was his chance! How he must have gripped his sword. If David had used his sword, that would have been unrighteous and not behaviour befitting a godly leader. Saul's office was of God. David reaches out with his sword and cuts off a part of Saul's robe (v 4) but signals to his men that he will not kill the Lord's anointed and prevents them from taking the law into their own hands (vv 6-7). He even seems to regret cutting the robe (v 5).

When Saul leaves the cave and David follows him out and calls after him (v 8), he shows deep dignity by calling him, "My lord the King". David explains to Saul that he could have killed him but chose not to. He shows Saul the strip of cloth he had cut from his coat and when Saul sees the cloth and hears David's words he begins to weep. Here is a special moment when God speaks to Saul, through the forbearance of David and an act of grace; as the Proverbs say, "A soft answer turneth away wrath" (Prov 15:1).

Saul acknowledges David's greatness in letting him go and accepts that David will be King. He pleads with David to not neglect his family when the time of his reign has come. This episode ends with David swearing to protect Saul's family, and so Saul leaves for the palace and David and his men go back to the hold (vv 16-22).

We feel sure that this act of restraint by David would have had mixed reviews in his camp. Some may have thought that one strike of his sword would have destroyed Saul once and for all. Some of his men (v 4) certainly thought that it was a God given opportunity for David to deal with Saul. Some might question David's courage as a result. Leaders need conviction about decision making or they will buckle under pressure. Godly leadership is based on actions which are pleasing to God and not necessarily following the popular mood. David is teaching the people that it is wrong to take the law into our own hands, and we cannot short circuit God's purpose no matter what pressure is placed upon us or how enticing circumstances are to do this. If God wants David as King, then He will bring it to pass (v 15). We may have to leave a company because we have been hounded out like David, but we are not at liberty to assassinate the leadership, irrespective of how carnal they are. This chapter speaks to us of the importance of forbearance and waiting on God's timing. Paul confirms that this is how we should behave today: "Put on therefore, as the elect of God, holy and beloved, bowels of mercies (compassion), kindness, humbleness of mind, meekness, longsuffering; Forbearing one another" (Col 3:12-13).

David also demonstrates the Lord's teaching for us all: "But I say unto you, Love your enemies, bless them that curse you, do good to them that hate you, and pray for them which despitefully use you, and persecute you; That ye may be the children of your Father which is in heaven: for he maketh his sun to rise on the evil and on the good, and sendeth rain on the just and on the unjust" (Matt 5:44-45). Our Lord Jesus was also a rejected King. Did they not say of Him "We have no king but Caesar" (John 19:15)? The hymn writer, Horatius Bonar, wrote these words which encourage us to walk in the steps of our Saviour:

"Go, labour on; spend, and be spent;
Thy joy to do the Father's will;
It is the way the Master went,
Should not the servant tread it still?"

The strip of cloth is a reminder to David of preservation from acting rashly. It reminded him of the old flesh within him and his natural desires which needed to be controlled. It was also a token of the future possession of the Kingdom. Just as Samuel's robe being cut was illustrative of the Kingdom being taken out of Saul's hand (1 Sam 15:27-28), so the piece of the King's robe showed that he had part of the Kingdom (600 men - 23:13) and the rest was yet to come. On the one hand the cloth signalled a great victory and, on the other hand, warned him of his own vulnerability. David had been one step away from disaster. People who live holy lives will still be tested. We are all painfully aware of how ugly the flesh is, but we can be given strength to have victory over it: "For the weapons of our warfare are not carnal, but mighty through God to the pulling down of strong holds" (2 Cor 10:4).

The sheathed sword at Carmel (Chapter 25)

Samuel dies at this point in David's life (v 1). Samuel was the man that had anointed David King. He had warned Saul that the Kingdom would be taken from him, and he had protected David from Saul through intercession (ch. 19). When good men die it can have a tremendous effect on those who know that the burden of responsibility is falling upon them. David is aware that he must be the next king, but the death of Samuel seems to have a mental unhinging on David. Death can sometimes do this to the most spiritual of believers. David begins to act out of character. The man that was so restrained in chapter 24 needs restrained himself in chapter 25. This chapter teaches us how we need to help our brother not to sin. James encourages us in this work: "Brethren, if any of you do err from the truth, and one convert him; Let him know, that he which converteth the sinner from the error of his way, shall save a soul from death, and shall hide a multitude of sins" (James 5:19-20).

When good men die, evil men often become more wicked. David and his men were living on the sides of Mount Carmel. Nabal owned the cattle on the mountain and was very rich (v 2). "Nabal" must have been his nickname describing his materialistic churlish character as it means "foolish". David and his men looked after the animals, protecting the sheep from thieves and wild beasts and he also protected Nabal's shepherds. When the lambing was all over and the shearing had commenced and the times of prosperity had come, David sent his men to Nabal looking for some kind of payment in kind. David's men were also hungry and looking for some kindness from Nabal (vv 5-9). Nabal refuses to give anything, speaking of "my bread, and my water, and my flesh that I have killed for my shearers" (v 11). He responds in a rage and in complete arrogance saying: "Who is David?" (vv 10-12).

It was one thing for David to say, "Who am I?" (2 Sam 7:18), but when Nabal says it, David loses patience. We need to remind ourselves of the danger of injured pride. Good men can fail and David, who had endured so much, is now losing his temper over one foolish man's attitude. The Hebrew writer reminds the persecuted saints that although they had endured so much, they must still be patient until the Lord comes: "For ye had compassion of me in my bonds, and took joyfully the spoiling of your goods, knowing in yourselves that ye have in heaven a better and an enduring substance. Cast not away therefore your confidence, which hath great recompence of reward. For ye have need of patience, that, after ye have done the will of God, ye might receive the promise. For yet a little while, and he that shall come will come, and will not tarry" (Heb 10:34-37). We are not in glory yet and we can all still fail, no matter what spiritual victories we have had in the past.

David in anger orders his men to gird on their swords and takes 400 people with him as he comes to judge Nabal (vv 13-14). It is at times like these that we need wise mediators and intercessors – often it is our sisters who show the most discernment, as did Abigail, Nabal's wife. Her intercessory prayers, reverence (she calls David "lord" 15 times), gracious request, and knowledge of David's previous conquests (vv 23-31) are in complete contrast to her aggressive husband who "flew at" David's servants (v 14). Her prophetic vision is astounding and is clearly spontaneous and authentic given her lack of preparation time (vv 28-29). She is demonstrating that conflict is never resolved in anger and her speed in intervening before David did himself damage shows the importance of nipping things in the bud and not allowing matters to fester and get worse. Abigail is hiding "a multitude of sins" (James 5:20).

We need "Abigails" who can intercede and persuade people to modify behaviours or reconsider actions. Into the midst of anger, miserly behaviour, injured pride and murderous thoughts come grace, wisdom, kindness and ultimately love. Only God can do this, and He often chooses to use His servants to do it. Are we available to be used in this way? Even the best of believers need recovered at some point in their life. Paul warns of the danger of us losing our temper: "But now ye also put off all these; anger, wrath, malice, blasphemy, filthy communication out of your mouth. Lie not one to another, seeing that ye have put off the old man with his deeds" (Col 3:8-9). Rather, Paul teaches the Colossians to "Put on therefore, as the elect of God, holy and beloved, bowels of mercies, kindness, humbleness of mind, meekness, longsuffering; Forbearing one another, and forgiving one another, if any man have a quarrel against any: even as Christ forgave you, so also do ye. And above all these things put on charity, which is the bond of perfectness" (Col 3:12-14). How many issues, splits and arguments could be avoided if we were to take to heart this teaching.

David is amazed at Abigail's intervention and foresight and tells her to go away in peace, as he turns back from his wicked intentions

(vv 32-35). Abigail goes home but does not tell Nabal because he is drunk, waiting instead until the morning. Nabal does not repent when he hears what has happened; his heart is hardened as a stone, and ten days later God judges him, and he dies (vv 36-38). This remarkable story ends with David marrying Abigail (vv 39-44). God will judge all evil and reward all good, but He often tests our character before He does this.

Saul's spear by his pillow in Ziph (Chapter 26)

Saul comes again after David into the wilderness of Ziph after the men of Ziph tell him where David is hiding (vv 1-3). This is his tenth recorded attempt on David's life by Saul (although there were many more attempts not recorded, see 23.14), and, as far as we know, this is the last. Ten is the number of responsibility, which is why we have Ten Commandments. Saul has failed completely in his responsibility. Some years before, Israel failed God ten times: "those men … have tempted me now these ten times, and have not hearkened to my voice" (Num 14:22-23). God said, "Enough"; none of the Israelites who had sinned were allowed to go into the land of Canaan as a result. After this tenth test which Saul fails, he has sealed his doom, and God will no longer speak to him. We often think that certain tests will never stop – but that is not true. God does eventually say, "Enough".

David and Abishai (Joab's brother) go down by night where Saul is camped. They find Saul asleep with his spear by his side and Abner, the captain of Saul's army, and the people surrounding him (v 7). Abishai again sees it as God's will to deliver Saul into their hands. He requests David to let him smite him and he adds that would not need to smite him a second time due to his accuracy (v 8). David refuses, reminding Abishai that he could not be guiltless if he touched the Lord's anointed, but added the Lord would smite Saul (vv 9-11). He initially asks Abishai to take his spear and his water skin from his pillow but it is interesting that David takes the spear himself (vv 11-12) perhaps to make sure Abishai was not tempted to use it on Saul. We need to be aware of the weaknesses of our brethren. We need to know when we can let men carry the spear: "Lay hands suddenly on no man, neither be partaker of other men's sins" (1 Tim 5.22). David and Abishai go across the valley to the hill opposite Hachilah and shout across to Abner and Saul in the night. Saul recognises the voice and again confesses that he has sinned and played the fool. David remarkably returns the spear and the water.

The spear that was flung at him at least three times he gave back to Saul – what grace! We cannot beat the flesh by acting with the flesh. It is when we have mastered the flesh by the power of the Spirit of God that we have the capacity to refuse to use its power; this is exemplified in Galatians: "Walk in the Spirit, and ye shall not fulfil the lust of the flesh. For the flesh lusteth against the Spirit, and the Spirit against the flesh: and these are contrary the one to the other: so that ye cannot do the things that ye would. But if ye be led of the Spirit, ye are not under the law" (Gal 5:16-19). Saul ends this conversation by telling David that he would be great and prevail. It is wonderful when even our enemies acknowledge the hand of God upon us.

We will be tested on areas where previously we have been victorious. There just might have been a nagging doubt from David that he missed his chance in chapter 24 and would not do so a second time. Sometimes the second test is more difficult than the first. But once again David has shown his true character. Clearly, forbearance is a value that God blesses. Patience will be rewarded, and, in God's time, His purposes will be made clear. David's conduct provides invaluable insight into how to deal with people whose behaviour is deplorable. We must always keep our dignity: "The servant of the Lord must not strive" (2 Tim 2:24).

The strip of cloth from Saul's clothes in chapter 24, the sheathed sword in chapter 25, and the spear returned to Saul in chapter 26 are all illustrative of the need of patience, self-control and forbearance in the things of God. In the days of his exile David is being taught something of God's character. Is He not patient with us?

PSALM 63

[A Psalm of David, when he was in the wilderness of Judah.]

¹ O God, thou art my God; early will I seek thee: my soul thirsteth for thee, my flesh longeth for thee in a dry and thirsty land, where no water is;

² To see thy power and thy glory, so as I have seen thee in the sanctuary.

³ Because thy lovingkindness is better than life, my lips shall praise thee.

⁴ Thus will I bless thee while I live: I will lift up my hands in thy name.

⁵ My soul shall be satisfied as with marrow and fatness; and my mouth shall praise thee with joyful lips:

⁶ When I remember thee upon my bed, and meditate on thee in the night watches.

⁷ Because thou hast been my help, therefore in the shadow of thy wings will I rejoice.

⁸ My soul followeth hard after thee: thy right hand upholdeth me.

⁹ But those that seek my soul, to destroy it, shall go into the lower parts of the earth.

¹⁰ They shall fall by the sword: they shall be a portion for foxes.

¹¹ But the king shall rejoice in God; every one that sweareth

by him shall glory: but the mouth of them that speak lies shall be stopped.

PSALM 116

Thanksgiving for deliverance from death

[1] I love the LORD, because he hath heard my voice and my supplications.

[2] Because he hath inclined his ear unto me, therefore will I call upon him as long as I live.

[3] The sorrows of death compassed me, and the pains of hell gat hold upon me: I found trouble and sorrow.

[4] Then called I upon the name of the LORD; O LORD, I beseech thee, deliver my soul.

[5] Gracious is the LORD, and righteous; yea, our God is merciful.

[6] The LORD preserveth the simple: I was brought low, and he helped me.

[7] Return unto thy rest, O my soul; for the LORD hath dealt bountifully with thee.

[8] For thou hast delivered my soul from death, mine eyes from tears, and my feet from falling.

[9] I will walk before the LORD in the land of the living.

¹⁰ I believed, therefore have I spoken: I was greatly afflicted:

¹¹ I said in my haste, All men are liars.

¹² What shall I render unto the LORD for all his benefits toward me?

¹³ I will take the cup of salvation, and call upon the name of the LORD.

¹⁴ I will pay my vows unto the LORD now in the presence of all his people.

¹⁵ Precious in the sight of the LORD is the death of his saints.

¹⁶ O LORD, truly I am thy servant; I am thy servant, and the son of thine handmaid: thou hast loosed my bonds.

¹⁷ I will offer to thee the sacrifice of thanksgiving, and will call upon the name of the LORD.

¹⁸ I will pay my vows unto the LORD now in the presence of all his people,

¹⁹ In the courts of the LORD'S house, in the midst of thee, O Jerusalem. Praise ye the LORD.

CHAPTER 9

David: His Calamity

1 Samuel 27-30

David moves from the wilderness of Ziph back to being with Achish, the king of Gath. The relentless attacks of Saul seem to be affecting David's spiritual equilibrium. Fear can drive us to do things we know in our hearts are wrong. These next chapters describe how David seems to win the favour of the Philistine king to the extent that he is given Ziklag, a Philistine city, to live in. It is during this time, when David is with Achish, that the Amalekites come and remove all David's possessions and his people and burn Ziklag with fire. When we are not walking with the Lord there is no saying what losses we will incur. This section ends, however, with David "recovering all" and it has lessons for us on recovery in the life of the believer.

Ziph to Ziklag (Chapter 27)

Living in fear can produce irrational behaviour that is out of character. These chapters are not David's finest hours as he spends 16 months (27:7) with Achish the Philistine king of Gath. He is effectively living a lie. David destroys the Amalekites and other enemies of God's people, but he claims to Achish that he is destroying Israelites loyal to King Saul. This impresses Achish and convinces him of David's loyalty. Sometimes God's people are found living a lie – saying one thing and doing another. We can look the part and say the right things but privately behave in a carnal and ungodly way. God hates this hypocrisy and will expose it. However, in David's case it was strangely the opposite of this. He behaved honourably but made out to a Philistine king that he was doing wicked deeds to Israel to be able to remain under his protection. Many a believer has failed here, living an honest life for the Lord but camouflaging their Christian faith when they are at work or at school to avoid persecution. God asks us to be courageous and be faithful to Him: "all that will live godly in Christ Jesus shall suffer persecution" (2 Tim 3:12).

In David's case it is a little more complicated than this. His masquerading is a direct result of persecution, and he was reasoning something like this: (i) he could not fight for King Saul; (ii) he would not fight for the Philistines; and so (iii) he would fight for the Lord and His people by being a fifth columnist in the camp of the Philistines, and when opportunity came he would turn against the Philistines and fight for God's people. The trouble is God never sanctions covert Christianity. Everybody who used disguise in the Bible were ultimately exposed – for example, Jacob (Gen 27), the Gibeonites (Josh 9), Saul (1 Sam 28), Jeroboam's wife (1 Kings 14), Ahab (1 Kings 22), and Josiah (2 Chron 35).

Achish is impressed with David's apparent opposition to King Saul and gives him the town of Ziklag to live in (27:5-6; 8-12). It proves that tribulation can bring its own form of trouble. He had gone to Achish before and escaped by the skin of his teeth having to feign madness (1 Sam 21), and now he has returned. Strangely, things seem to be working out. Achish is showing David favour. When the world starts showing us favour, we need to look out! These chapters show we should never assume that apparent success means that God is smiling on our sin - it is just God's forbearance and grace. At Ziklag they will lose everything (ch 30)! God does sometimes allow certain choices we make in order for us to learn lessons, but then He intervenes in our lives to bring us to our senses. Thankfully, this section concludes with David recovering all at Ziklag. He will learn the truth of recovery, but not before he has known what it is to lose everything! Ziklag is well named, meaning to press someone or something to reveal what is inside. The word was used to produce metal from ore, a smeltery. In that sense it certainly was true of David - he was tested to the core at Ziklag.

Jeremiah was told to preach to Israel: "See, I have this day set thee over the nations and over the kingdoms, to root out, and to pull down, and to destroy, and to throw down, to build, and to plant" (Jer 1:10)

- four negative things and then two positive things. We have to know what it is to pull down before we know what it is to plant. Do we have a tolerance zone in the assembly, or in our lives, of something we know needs to be pulled down? There is a breaking down before there can be a building up. It is often loss before recovery.

Going to war - Ziklag to Shunem (Chapter 28)

So why is David not at Ziklag when the Amalekites attack in 1 Samuel 30? The reason is that a war is emerging with all the Lords of the Philistines against King Saul, and Achish is determined that David will fight alongside his men. Saul and his forces are in Gilboa on the edge of the Esdraelon valley and the Philistines are gathering in Shumen on the northern edge of the Jezreel valley, some ten miles from Saul's army (28:1-4). The presence of God has left Saul and God does not speak to him via dreams, visions, Urim or by prophets (28:6). Instead, Saul seeks counsel of a witch at Endor with disastrous consequences – the full story is given in the remainder of chapter 28. It is a salutary lesson as Saul the man who stood head and shoulders above the people resorts to witchcraft. Oh, the sadness of those who get away from the Lord; there is no saying how far they will fall.

Being sent home - Aphek to Ziklag (Chapter 29)

The Philistines begin to move their troops forward to Aphek and that is when the other Lords of the Philistines realise that David and his army were with them. This becomes a matter of internal conflict between the five Lords of the Philistines and Achish. The Lord of Gath makes it clear to David that he must leave with his men immediately at dawn the next day (ch 29). David's big plan was probably to kill the Philistines in the heat of battle and perhaps win the hearts and minds of the nation of Israel, but it all comes to nothing. We cannot do God's work using carnal methods (2 Cor 10:4). God will never sanction fifth columnists in worldly pursuits or covert Christianity as an approach to evangelism; His method is to publicly "preach the Word".

Back at Ziklag (Chapter 30)

The sorrow (vv 1-5): When we know we have failed

When they return to Ziklag they discover it is burned with fire and all their wives and children have been kidnapped. There has been an Amalekite invasion when they have been away. The sadness of these verses cannot be overstated. Amalek, an old enemy, attacked and destroyed everything. We first read of him in Exodus 17. Amalek is a picture of the flesh – our lifelong enemy. As Moses said: "the LORD hath sworn that the LORD will have war with Amalek from generation to generation" (Ex 17:16). Paul confirms we have a daily battle with the old flesh until the Lord comes or we are taken to be with Christ: "For the flesh lusteth against the Spirit, and the Spirit against the flesh: and these are contrary the one to the other: so that ye cannot do the things that ye would" (Gal 5:17). It is only in the power of the Holy Spirit we can overcome.

The Amalekites are bandits. Their intelligence told them that David was fighting with the Philistines 70 miles away and so now was the time to attack. Amalek always appears when we are feeble (Ex 17:7-8) and often takes the weakest, just as he attacked the women and children here. In the wilderness Amalek attacked from the rear and took out those on the periphery and those who were finding the way difficult. This is why victory over Amalek is so important. Israel were instructed: "Remember what Amalek did unto thee by the way, when ye were come forth out of Egypt; How he met thee by the way, and smote the hindmost of thee, even all that were feeble behind thee, when thou wast faint and weary; and he feared not God. Therefore, it shall be, when the LORD thy God hath given thee rest from all thine enemies round about, in the land which the LORD thy God giveth thee for an inheritance to possess it, that thou shalt blot out the remembrance of Amalek from under heaven; thou shalt not forget it" (Deut 25:17-19). The flesh, like Amalek, always attacks when we are unsuspecting, and when we are vulnerable. Ill health, family issues, assembly problems are fertile territory for an attack. The answer lies in not leaving ourselves "wide open" as David left Ziklag unprotected. Paul says: "But put ye on the Lord Jesus Christ, and make not provision for the flesh, to fulfil the lusts thereof" (Rom 13:14).

It so solemn to read that "their wives, and their sons, and their daughters, were taken captives" (v 3). Very often when we fail it is our families and our wives that are affected the most! The collateral damage of our failure cannot be overstated. Lot's choice of Sodom had a disastrous impact on his family (Gen chs 13-19). "Good understanding giveth favour: but the way of transgressors is hard" (Prov 13:15). No wonder David and his men "lifted up their voice and wept, until they had no more power to weep" (v 4). This is the sorrow of sin! But we have all been there. We all need to get there. "For godly sorrow worketh repentance to salvation not to be repented of: but the sorrow of the world worketh death" (2 Cor 7:10). God blesses when His people show real sorrow. Our prayer meetings should reflect this. Do we not feel the collective sense of loss today? Nehemiah did (Neh 1:7), David did, we all should. It is the start of the road to blessing. In some ways the Amalekites had become the instruments of discipline by God.

The strengthening (vv 6-8): When we make matters worse

Sometimes, when the saints are in a crisis, we can make matters worse as happened here: "And David was greatly distressed; for the people spake of stoning him, because the soul of all the people was grieved, every man for his sons and for his daughters" (v 6). They started blaming David for leaving the city unguarded. You can almost feel the animosity - someone's head has to roll, and it would be David's! We blame people when things go wrong. It is so sad when the assembly is going through difficulty that people start blaming and fighting and making matters worse. A common reaction in the wilderness when times were tough was to take up stones to stone the leader Moses (e.g. Ex 17:4)! Good leaders can become *persona non grata*. Grief can make people behave like animals! But it is not good enough. David was in desperate straits. It says he was "greatly distressed". Our leaders are humans, our shepherds are sheep, and they have feelings like us. We need to support them not stone them. The great general David who attracted hundreds to share his exile in Adullam was now isolated from his own troops. He had lost everything, including his wives and children, and now he had lost the loyalty of his men. David is at rock bottom. What is the solution?

- **Encouragement: Leaning on the Lord alone for encouragement**

Scripture simply but wonderfully says: "... but David encouraged himself in the LORD his God" (v 6). Sometimes the attack of Amalek is how a person is recovered to the Lord. David looks solely to the Lord and depends on no human resource. Sometimes, when we are stripped bare, we realise that we are totally dependent on the Lord for protection It is when we are "weak" we are strong. Paul learned this, possibly in the extremity of a stoning in Galatia that almost killed him: "And he said unto me, My grace is sufficient for thee: for my strength is made perfect in weakness. Most gladly therefore will I rather glory in my infirmities, that the power of Christ may rest upon me" (2 Cor 12:9).

- **Consolation: Learning to draw on priestly ministry**

It is here in this place of casting himself upon God that "David said to Abiathar the priest, Ahimelech's son, I pray thee, bring me hither the ephod" (v 7). A strengthened saint realises the importance of priestly men and of drawing near to God. We have a "great high priest" in heaven who sympathises with us and encourages us to draw near to the "throne of grace" that we might obtain mercy and find grace to help in our hour of need (Heb 4:14-16).

- **Intercession and Enquiry: Looking to the Lord for guidance**

David asks for guidance before making up his mind about pursuing: "And David enquired at the LORD, saying, Shall I pursue after this troop? shall I overtake them?" (v 8). David remembers how God guided him at Keilah and so he intercedes. He later composed a Psalm and wrote of God: "I will instruct thee and teach thee in the way which thou shalt go: I will guide thee with mine eye" (Ps 32:8).

- **Guidance and strength: Living by His promises.**

God says "Pursue, and "thou shalt ... without fail recover all" (v 8). What a promise. Prayer strengthens us. Paul says: "For this cause I bow my knees unto the Father of our Lord Jesus Christ, Of whom the whole family in heaven and earth is named, That he would grant you, according to the riches of his glory, to be strengthened with might by his Spirit in the inner man" (Eph 3:14-16). Let us not forget the critical resource of prayer to strengthen us in dire circumstances.

The Succouring (vv 9-16): Tested on the route to recovery

The expressions "So David went" (v 9), and "David pursued" (v 10) are heartening. He was acting on God's promise: "... thou shalt surely overtake them, and without fail recover all"

Acting on God's promises is where we see the blessing. There are so many injunctions in Scripture, and when we act on them, we will be blessed; for example, "Preach the Word". The question is, are we acting on His Word?

They had marched 70 miles in three days from Aphek to Ziklag only to find no provisions there. David leaves two hundred behind, "which were so faint that they could not go over the brook Besor" (v 10). Taking into account the various strengths of our brothers and sisters is required if there is to be recovery. Epaphroditus almost died ministering to Paul's needs: "Yet I supposed it necessary to send to you Epaphroditus, my brother, and companion in labour, and fellow soldier, but your messenger, and he that ministered to my wants. For he longed after you all, and was full of heaviness, because that ye had heard that he had been sick. For indeed he was sick nigh unto death: but God had mercy on him; and not on him only, but on me also, lest I should have sorrow upon sorrow. I sent him therefore the more carefully, that, when ye see him again, ye may rejoice, and that I may be the less sorrowful. Receive him therefore in the Lord with all gladness; and hold such in reputation: Because for the work of Christ he was nigh unto death, not regarding his life, to supply your lack of service toward me" (Phil 2:25-30). Let us show real care when our brethren are losing strength.

It was as they were rushing to recover their wives and children from the Amalekites that "they found an Egyptian in the field, and brought him to David" (v 11). He had been abandoned for being weak (v 13). We are sure many would have been saying that they were running for their wives and children and could not stop for a weak Egyptian slave! But David deals with him as the Good Samaritan dealt with the man at the side of the road, half dead (Luke 10), giving him "bread, and he did eat; and they made him drink water; And they gave him a piece of a cake of figs, and two clusters of raisins" (vv 11-12) Our love for others, even our enemies, is part of the recovery process. Later David would write, "Blessed is he that considereth the poor" (Ps 41:1). The Hebrew writer adds: "Be not forgetful to entertain strangers: for thereby some have entertained angels unawares" (Heb 13:2). Paul simply says "And be ye kind" (Eph 4:32). The reward from the Lord was that the Egyptian slave led them straight to the Amalekites: "And when he had brought him down, behold, they were spread abroad upon all the earth, eating and drinking, and dancing, because of all the great spoil that they had taken out of the land of the Philistines, and out of the land of Judah" (v 16). God always blesses kindness, particularly when it is directed to those who have been adversely affected by the behaviour of others.

The Salvation (vv 17-19): Recovery!

When the Amalekites least expect it, David and his men descend upon them. David waits until they are weak and drunk after a day and night of revelry, then throughout the night destroys them whilst preserving all their prisoners. The merriment of the Amalekites had replaced military discipline. David never lost a war and in that sense is a reminder of our Saviour the Lord Jesus. Just as it says here that "there escaped not a man" (v 17), so we learn from Paul that when the Saviour comes in judgment: "they shall not escape' (1 Thess 5:3). It is "a righteous thing with God to recompense tribulation to them that trouble you" (2 Thess 1:6).

- **Recovery of all: The goodness of God**

    Just as God had said in verse 8 that they would "without fail recover all", so verse 18 wonderfully states that "David recovered all". There is nothing like recovery. Often times there are losses, but here the recovery was absolutely complete. It reminds us of the Lord's words in relation to our salvation: "And this is the Father's will which hath sent me, that of all which he hath given me I should lose nothing" (John 6:39). Truly we can say with the Psalmist David that "He restoreth my soul" (Psalm 23:3). To be involved in the restoration of saints in any way is a wonderful privilege (James 5:20; Gal 6:1). All the sorrow has turned to joy.

The Spoil (vv 20-31): Wisdom after recovery

We can spoil things after a day of victory and recovery (vv 20-22). When we start to analyse who played the greatest part in the victory and naming and shaming those who appeared to do less, it is a sign that Amalek's legacy is with us. Often after victories the joy of success is tempered by pride. It happened after Gideon's famous victory over the Midianites. The greed of human nature clouded one of Israel's brightest days as Ephraim seemed envious that the victory did not involve them. "And the men of Ephraim said unto him, Why hast thou served us thus, that thou calledst us not, when thou wentest to fight with the Midianites? And they did chide with him sharply" (Judges 8:1). This type of behaviour needs to be corrected. That is why Moses wrote about what they should do with the spoils of war after victory, for example, following the defeat of the Midianites (Num 31:25-54; and more generally in Deut 20:10-15). The lesson is simply this, the "battle is the Lord's" and the spoils of victory must be equally shared. God's goodness to us should result in goodness to others.

David is crystal clear in this: all must get an equal share in the spoil: "as his part is that goeth down to the battle, so shall his part be that tarrieth by the stuff: they shall part alike. And it was so from that day forward, that he made it a statute and an ordinance for Israel unto this day" (vv 24-25). David had seen first-hand the results of praising one man more than another in public when the women sang of Saul slaying his thousands and David his tens of thousands (1 Sam 18). It resulted in terrible envy. We need to ensure that at all times we are marked by equity in the way we pass out praise or finance.

David takes time to send on a share of the spoils of war to the elders of Judah; to 14 cities in total, he sent "a present" (vv 26-31). These were places that had looked after him (v 31) when he was being chased by Saul, and, while David could not recompense them then, he rewards them now. We need to remember this when we feel impoverished in our service for the Lord - we will be fully rewarded in a coming day (2 Tim 4:6-8). When we are blessed, we should give, unlike Nabal the Carmelite (1 Sam 25). The chapter starts with David grieving and ends with him giving. The man that lived in caves is now very rich. If, when we have, we give to those who are in need, then when we are in need we will be looked after. We never know who we are helping each day - we might be entertaining angels unawares. "God is not unrighteous to forget your work and labour of love, which ye have shewed toward his name, in that ye have ministered to the saints, and do minister" (Heb 6:10).

PSALM 4

[To the chief Musician on Neginoth, A Psalm of David]

¹ Hear me when I call, O God of my righteousness: thou hast enlarged me when I was in distress; have mercy upon me, and hear my prayer.

² O ye sons of men, how long will ye turn my glory into shame? how long will ye love vanity, and seek after leasing? Selah.

³ But know that the LORD hath set apart him that is godly for himself: the LORD will hear when I call unto him.

⁴ Stand in awe, and sin not: commune with your own heart upon your bed, and be still. Selah.

⁵ Offer the sacrifices of righteousness, and put your trust in the LORD.

⁶ There be many that say, Who will shew us any good? LORD, lift thou up the light of thy countenance upon us.

⁷ Thou hast put gladness in my heart, more than in the time that their corn and their wine increased.

⁸ I will both lay me down in peace, and sleep: for thou, LORD, only makest me dwell in safety.

CHAPTER 10

David: His Cry

1 Samuel 31 - 2 Samuel 2

These chapters tell of the deaths of Saul and Jonathan at the hands of the Philistines, and David's response when he hears the tragic news. Saul and his sons are killed by the Philistines on Mount Gilboa at the eastern end of the Jezreel valley (also called Esdraelon or Armageddon). It would seem likely that the archers wounded them, and it was only after the war was over that the Philistines discovered that they had been slain. The primary sources describing Saul's death are found in 1 Samuel 31 and 1 Chronicles 10. Saul, mortally injured, falls on his own sword and his armour bearer, after seeing that Saul is dead, falls on his sword too. David learns of these events from an opportunistic Amalekite who adds various colourful details to the narrative, including the fact that he, the Amalekite, had killed Saul (2 Sam 1). David is deeply moved when he hears of their deaths, composing a funeral song of memorial to be taught to all the families in Israel. He feels keenly the loss in the kingdom. He slays the Amalekite for claiming to have killed Saul, showing at this moment that he is honourable and not seeking the throne for the throne's sake. Our true character will always be seen by how we react when our enemy is destroyed. The tenderness of David's heart is manifest, and his love for others is greater than any thought of self-advancement.

The death of Israel's first king at Armageddon stands in contrast to Israel's last and final King who will come and demolish all the enemies of God at Armageddon as recorded for us in Revelation 16:16 and chapter 19. Zechariah prophesies of the Lord Jesus' victory in Ephraim (location of Armageddon) and in Jerusalem when He returns as King: "And I will cut off the chariot from Ephraim, and the horse from Jerusalem, and the battle bow shall be cut off: and he shall speak peace unto the heathen: and his dominion shall be from sea even to sea, and from the river even to the ends of the earth" (Zech 9:10). The kingdom of Christ shall have "no end" (Luke 1:33).

David begins to take possession of the Kingdom in these chapters as they map his transition from Ziklag to Hebron. David has known loss and full recovery at Ziklag, and yet, as he hears of the crumbling Kingdom, his heart is moved. The moment has come for him to be accepted as King. As already noted in chapter nine, Ziklag means to press someone or something to reveal what is inside, and is also used to describe the production of metal from ore, a smeltery. This is so fitting a meaning as we think of the crucible of the testing David received there in 1 Samuel 30. "Hebron" means to join, i.e. the place of fellowship. Again, this is an appropriate name. Here, David is going to be crowned King, people will come and acknowledge his leadership, and there will be unity and healing. So how does David go from the place of pressing and testing to the place of joining, healing, and fellowshipping? The aspects of the behaviour that David exhibits teach us lessons when we go through periods of transition in our lives and in the life of the assembly.

Calmness (2 Sam 1:1-12)

In days of incredible weakness, a son of Amalek arrives (2 Sam 1:1-12) and seeks to wheedle his way into the camp of Israel. David handles him with a calm and measured spirit, listening to his story and questioning carefully. He did not allow himself to get too excited, and he was not gullible as the Amalekite related his fictitious account of Saul's death.

In days of weakness, Amalek (that picture of the flesh) can arrive and seek entry into the assembly. As Christians we must be on our guard when we are brought news which seems suspicious. Paul pre-warned the saints in Ephesus: "For I know this, that after my departing shall grievous wolves enter in among you, not sparing the flock" (Acts 20:29). Days of smallness and weakness are days of great vulnerability.

In Zerubbabel's day there were those who claimed to be priests but could not prove their connection to the priesthood and so they were rejected (Ezra 2:61-63). In such a day of smallness it must have been painful to not receive them. We can clutch at straws because someone is showing an interest. It needs calm minds and hearts and wisdom to know the difference between those who are genuinely seeking and charlatans who have ulterior motives. Hasty decisions have ruined assemblies. Amalek always comes when we are weak (Ex 17:7-8).

We can, of course, have the opposite problem. We should not be needlessly suspicious people. We should get excited when someone gets saved or someone is restored. We should give people the benefit of the doubt and be marked by cautious optimism. But this behaviour by David is reminding us to judge what someone says by the way they live their lives. Paul similarly counselled Timothy: "Lay hands suddenly on no man" (1 Tim 5:22). In other words, do not be over hasty to put people in positions of authority, unless their gift is backed up by a consistent Christian testimony.

Discerning (2 Sam 1:13-16)

However, it is also true that our words can give insight into our character. The light tongue of the Amalekite shows a lack of appreciation for David's deep-seated conviction about Saul's God-given authority, a lack of reverence for God's honour, and a lack of respect for the office of the King, God's anointed. He nonchalantly said, "So I stood upon him, and slew him ... and I took the crown that was upon his head, and the bracelet that was on his arm, and have brought them hither unto my lord" (1:10). He assumed that David was a person like him – an opportunist and anxious to be promoted at any cost. The Amalekite anticipated that David would have been pleased that Saul was dead. He was not. The true character of David shows remarkable discernment here as is seen in his response to his enemy's misfortune.

In the previous chapter we saw Amalek as a picture of the flesh. It is not without significance that King Saul, who would not slay Agag the Amalekite (1 Sam 15:3, 9, 22), is now stripped of his crown by an Amalekite. Sparing the flesh is always a disaster, and in Saul's case it confirms that the flesh, if spared, does not spare us. There is only one way to deal with the flesh and that is to reckon it dead (Rom 6:11; Gal 5:24) and to actively "mortify" the deeds of the body, that is put them to death (Rom 6:12-14; 8:13); perhaps David's slaying of the Amalekite is a metaphor for this (2 Sam 1:14-16).

Care (2 Sam 1:17)

David really cared. His lamentation over the news about the death of Saul and Jonathan was real. We all can follow a man who has a compassionate heart. A shepherd heart is crucial if people are going to follow anyone. The Lord Jesus, the greatest leader this world has ever known, was marked by a compassionate heart: "But when he saw the multitudes, he was moved with compassion on them, because they fainted, and were scattered abroad, as sheep having no shepherd" (Matt 9:36). It was He who commissioned Peter as a shepherd, but first He tested his heart and his affections: "Simon, son of Jonas, lovest thou me? Peter was grieved because he said unto him the third time, Lovest thou me? And he said unto him, Lord, thou knowest all things; thou knowest that I love thee. Jesus saith unto him, Feed my sheep" (John 21:17). The Lord still commissions people with shepherd hearts.

Learning (2 Sam 1:18)

A spirit which is open to teaching is critical in days of transition. Good leaders are known for learning lessons from defeat. David was determined to learn lessons from the downfall of Saul and Jonathan. He instructed the leaders to teach the people the bow song which he had composed and recorded in a book. He wanted the tragedy to teach them lessons. It would look as if Saul lost out strategically to the Philistine archers (1 Sam 31:3). The battle of Gilboa was really the battle of Jezreel on the edge of the vast Esdraelon plain. The Philistines had many chariots (1 Sam 13:5) and they brought a host of cavalry that Israel could not match. Israel fled into the mountain of Gilboa, but the Philistine military strategists were prepared for this and unleashed their archers against Saul and his fleeing soldiers. It was these bows and arrows that killed Saul and his sons. David teaches a song of mourning and also a song of learning about the bow. The bow was the very weapon with which David knew Jonathan was so skilled (1 Sam 20:36) - it is about keeping the enemy at a distance! Perhaps we need to learn the strategic lesson of keeping ourselves at a distance from our enemies. Christians ought not to put themselves in positions of vulnerability: "abstain from fleshly lusts, which war against the soul" (1 Peter 2:11). The world wants us to come down to its level and enjoy its places of entertainment – it is a danger zone. If we are to stay safe, we need to wear the large shield of faith for protection. As Paul exhorts: "Wherefore, take unto you the whole armour of God, that ye may be able to withstand in the evil day, and having done all, to stand … Above all, taking the shield of faith, wherewith ye shall be able to quench all the fiery darts of the wicked" (Eph 6:13-16).

Generosity (2 Sam 1:19)

Leaders are known for their generosity of spirit. The importance of being able to see the good in previous leaders is critical in times of transition. Those who pour scorn on guides of the past learn that such an approach backfires. David describes Saul as "The beauty of Israel" and acknowledges him as a valiant soldier slain in the high places of Gilboa. He exclaims, "… how are the mighty fallen!" and this description of "mighty" included Saul, the same Saul who had acted so wretchedly towards David! It is sad when we cannot see any good in people and a critical spirit is all too easily found in us.

Whilst David personally had been negatively affected by Saul, for many he (Saul) had brought stability and a measure of prosperity to the country. David says, "Ye daughters of Israel, weep over Saul, who clothed you in scarlet, with other delights, who put on ornaments of gold upon your apparel" (2 Sam 1:24). Leaders can see the wider picture. Saul had been a valiant man and so had Jonathan, even if at times David felt that Saul's war mongering had been misplaced.

Whilst David knew that Jonathan had remonstrated on his behalf with his father on more than one occasion, he also knew that Jonathan had been loyal to his father and served him faithfully. Father and son were even joined together in death (2 Sam 1:23). This unity with the royal family brought stability to the Kingdom. It is good when we can see that someone has blessed others even if we have not been within the scope of their benevolence.

We should, therefore, try hard to look for the best in everyone, even in those of who have wronged us. When Paul writes to Philemon about his runaway slave he writes with such dignity: "Onesimus, a faithful and beloved brother, who is one of you" (Col 4:9). When Paul speaks to Timothy of Mark, who had left Paul on his first missionary journey and was instrumental in a rift between Paul and Barnabas, he does so with such grace: "Take Mark, and bring him with thee: for he is profitable to me for the ministry" (2 Tim 4:11).

David maybe taught Solomon this proverb, but even if not, he lived it out: "Rejoice not when thine enemy falleth, and let not thine heart be glad when he stumbleth" (Prov 24:17). Delighting in another's misfortune will never help any healing in a time of transition.

Confidentiality (2 Sam 1:20)

Leaders are known for their discreet behaviour when discussing failure. We should not allow the ungodly to hear about the failures of fellow saints. David laments: "Tell it not in Gath, publish it not in the streets of Askelon; lest the daughters of the Philistines rejoice, lest the daughters of the uncircumcised triumph". He really did not want this tragic loss to be known amongst the Philistines. It reminds us of the Saviour's words: "Give not that which is holy unto the dogs, neither cast ye your pearls before swine, lest they trample them under their feet, and turn again and rend you" (Matt 7:6). We must never talk disparagingly about the saints to the unsaved or even allude to any issue of doctrinal difference. Another proverb David might have taught Solomon could be: "A talebearer revealeth secrets: but he that is of a faithful spirit concealeth the matter" (Prov 11:13).

This song was known hundreds of years later in the prophet Micah's day (Micah 1:10). The song should be proverbial in our generation. We must know the "bow song" and how to keep our distance, keep our focus on good things, and keep our counsel!

Love (2 Sam 1:25-27)

David's love for Jonathan is very moving: "I am distressed for thee, my brother Jonathan: very pleasant hast thou been unto me: thy love to me was wonderful, passing the love of women" (2 Sam 1:26). Christianity is marked by true love – this love is beyond the natural love of, for example, a husband to a wife (1 John 5:1). As a relatively young man Jonathan had taken his robe and his bow and given them to David and acknowledged him as leader (1 Sam 18:4). Jonathan had spoken up for David to his father thus allowing David to be restored to his position (1 Sam 19). Jonathan had secretly advised David to run, ensured David was not caught by his father, and promised that he (Jonathan) would always look after him and his family (1 Sam 20). He had come to the forest of Hachilah and had endangered his own life to strengthen David's hand in God (1 Sam 23). He had forfeited his claim to the throne, and his relationship with his father, all for David. David never forgot it. Jonathan was willing to see the greatness in David and tragically thought he could turn the Kingdom to David, but he could not - if only he had left to be with David. Part of the tears here are the regret David had about Jonathan.

Love is the oil of healing in days of transition and is the lubricant of any change. People need to know they are loved.

Prayer (2 Sam 2:1-3)

Times of transition require us all to turn to God for guidance. Leaders are known for their intercession and seeking the mind of God. David certainly showed us the importance of this as he enquired after the Lord whether he should go to Hebron. He had learned at Keilah (1 Sam 23) that when he enquired of the Lord, the Lord guided him, and he had learned at Ziklag (1 Sam 30) that when he enquired of the Lord, the Lord led him, and he recovered all. He is learning once again in a time of loss to enquire of the Lord, and the Lord guides him to reign in Hebron.

David walks the 18 miles north-east from Ziklag to Hebron. Hebron is 20 miles south-west of Jerusalem on the main road to Beersheba. It had previously been called Kirjatharba (Gen 23:2), then a royal Canaanite city (Josh 10:3, 5), was taken from the Anakims and given to Caleb and his posterity, and became a city of refuge. It was a place of great nostalgia to David - his two wives came from these parts - Ahinoam the Jezreelitess, and Abigail the Carmelitess (Josh 15:55-56; 1 Sam 27:3).

Patience (2 Sam 2:4)

Transition periods need patience. The anointing of David as King over Judah had been a long time coming. Many might feel, reading the narrative of 1 Samuel, that it was far too long, but effective leaders need to be patient. Impatience creates tension and does not develop unity. Now that David would be King, he would be glad that he did not kill Saul in 1 Samuel 24 or in 1 Samuel 26. James says: "... the trying of your faith worketh patience" (James 1:3). Was it here that David wrote Psalm 18: "... thy gentleness hath made me great", and again, "Great deliverance giveth he to his king; and sheweth mercy to his anointed, to David" (vv 35, 50)? His Kingdom would be all the better for his lack of interference in his own promotion. The crowning day is coming by and by for all of us. There is not a trace of bitterness in David. We need to pray that the "root of bitterness" does not spring up and trouble us (Heb 12:15) - "For ye have need of patience, that, after ye have done the will of God, ye might receive the promise" (Heb 10:36). On the other hand, may we be like the men of Judah, ready to acknowledge the gift given to others and follow those who seek the good of God's people.

PSALM 18

*[To the chief Musician, A Psalm of David, the servant of the
LORD, who spake unto the LORD the words of this song in
the day that the LORD delivered him from the hand of all
his enemies, and from the hand of Saul: And he said,]*

¹ I will love thee, O LORD, my strength.

² The LORD is my rock, and my fortress, and my deliverer;
my God, my strength, in whom I will trust; my buckler, and
the horn of my salvation, and my high tower.

³ I will call upon the LORD, who is worthy to be praised: so
shall I be saved from mine enemies.

⁴ The sorrows of death compassed me, and the floods of
ungodly men made me afraid.

⁵ The sorrows of hell compassed me about: the snares of
death prevented me.

⁶ In my distress I called upon the LORD, and cried unto my
God: he heard my voice out of his temple, and my cry came
before him, even into his ears.

⁷ Then the earth shook and trembled; the foundations also
of the hills moved and were shaken, because he was wroth.

⁸ There went up a smoke out of his nostrils, and fire out of
his mouth devoured: coals were kindled by it.

⁹ He bowed the heavens also, and came down: and darkness
was under his feet.

¹⁰ And he rode upon a cherub, and did fly: yea, he did fly
upon the wings of the wind.

[11] He made darkness his secret place; his pavilion round about him were dark waters and thick clouds of the skies.

[12] At the brightness that was before him his thick clouds passed, hail stones and coals of fire.

[13] The LORD also thundered in the heavens, and the Highest gave his voice; hail stones and coals of fire.

[14] Yea, he sent out his arrows, and scattered them; and he shot out lightnings, and discomfited them.

[15] Then the channels of waters were seen, and the foundations of the world were discovered at thy rebuke, O LORD, at the blast of the breath of thy nostrils.

[16] He sent from above, he took me, he drew me out of many waters.

[17] He delivered me from my strong enemy, and from them which hated me: for they were too strong for me.

[18] They prevented me in the day of my calamity: but the LORD was my stay.

[19] He brought me forth also into a large place; he delivered me, because he delighted in me.

[20] The LORD rewarded me according to my righteousness; according to the cleanness of my hands hath he recompensed me.

[21] For I have kept the ways of the LORD, and have not wickedly departed from my God.

[22] For all his judgments were before me, and I did not put away his statutes from me.

[23] I was also upright before him, and I kept myself from mine iniquity.

[24] Therefore hath the LORD recompensed me according to

my righteousness, according to the cleanness of my hands in his eyesight.

25 With the merciful thou wilt shew thyself merciful; with an upright man thou wilt shew thyself upright;

26 With the pure thou wilt shew thyself pure; and with the froward thou wilt shew thyself froward.

27 For thou wilt save the afflicted people; but wilt bring down high looks.

28 For thou wilt light my candle: the LORD my God will enlighten my darkness.

29 For by thee I have run through a troop; and by my God have I leaped over a wall.

30 As for God, his way is perfect: the word of the LORD is tried: he is a buckler to all those that trust in him.

31 For who is God save the LORD? or who is a rock save our God?

32 It is God that girdeth me with strength, and maketh my way perfect.

33 He maketh my feet like hinds' feet, and setteth me upon my high places.

34 He teacheth my hands to war, so that a bow of steel is broken by mine arms.

35 Thou hast also given me the shield of thy salvation: and thy right hand hath holden me up, and thy gentleness hath made me great.

36 Thou hast enlarged my steps under me, that my feet did not slip.

37 I have pursued mine enemies, and overtaken them: neither did I turn again till they were consumed.

³⁸ I have wounded them that they were not able to rise: they are fallen under my feet.

³⁹ For thou hast girded me with strength unto the battle: thou hast subdued under me those that rose up against me.

⁴⁰ Thou hast also given me the necks of mine enemies; that I might destroy them that hate me.

⁴¹ They cried, but there was none to save them: even unto the LORD, but he answered them not.

⁴² Then did I beat them small as the dust before the wind: I did cast them out as the dirt in the streets.

⁴³ Thou hast delivered me from the strivings of the people; and thou hast made me the head of the heathen: a people whom I have not known shall serve me.

⁴⁴ As soon as they hear of me, they shall obey me: the strangers shall submit themselves unto me.

⁴⁵ The strangers shall fade away, and be afraid out of their close places.

⁴⁶ The LORD liveth; and blessed be my rock; and let the God of my salvation be exalted.

⁴⁷ It is God that avengeth me, and subdueth the people under me.

⁴⁸ He delivereth me from mine enemies: yea, thou liftest me up above those that rise up against me: thou hast delivered me from the violent man.

⁴⁹ Therefore will I give thanks unto thee, O LORD, among the heathen, and sing praises unto thy name.

⁵⁰ Great deliverance giveth he to his king; and sheweth mercy to his anointed, to David, and to his seed for evermore.

CHAPTER 11

David: His Crowning
2 Samuel 2-5

Chapters 2-5 describe the coronation of David as King over Judah and then eventually over all Israel. It is a period in his life that deals with the dangers of transitions and exemplifies types of leadership behaviour that are essential for effective rule.

The journey from Hebron (chapter 2) to Jerusalem (chapter 5) takes place over these chapters. Hebron is 20 miles southwest of Jerusalem on the main road to Beersheba. This particular journey is the transition from partial recovery to full recovery, from the commencement of fellowship to full unity across the nation. David has been crowned King of Judah but not King of Israel in 2 Samuel 2. Only Judah has been loyal to him, although multitudes came to him from many tribes, as is recorded for us in 1 Chronicles 12. David's leadership is only acknowledged partially and not fully by the whole nation, for political purposes. Abner (Saul's former captain) makes Saul's only surviving son, Ishbosheth, king over Israel. Ishbosheth lasted two years before he died, but it was seven and a half years before David was crowned King over all Israel (2 Sam 2:8-11; 5:4-5). David never became King of Judah by force, and he would not become King of Israel by force. People who will lead God's people do not take a position of leadership by force. We are reminded of Peter's words: "... taking the oversight thereof, not by constraint, but willingly; not for filthy lucre, but of a ready mind" (1 Peter 5:2). Those who force their way into positions of leadership often prove to be false.

However, things are not in a good position until the whole nation is unified. People are in places of power who are unfitted. They have been coerced into it, like Ishbosheth. Weak people are in positions of power because of strong connections. We also have pragmatists and pugilists like Abner and Joab - powerful individuals who know how to manipulate people for personal profit. The New Testament says that one of the characteristic features of an elder in an Assembly of God's people should be "no striker, not greedy of filthy lucre; but patient, not a brawler, not covetous" (1 Tim 3:3).

Abner (Ishbosheth's army captain) and Joab (David's army captain) call for a wrestling match between the 12 best young men on both sides which results in a blood bath (2 Samuel 2) and the death of Asahel, Joab's brother. Quite often the casualties of such aggressive men are our young people and a future generation. Things can be done in periods of transition that result in long-standing feuds.

Thankfully there are people like David who are true shepherds who can unite God's people. Although there is much that might not be right, with God's help unity can be established from the most unlikely of starting points. We do not provoke fights with people who are unfitted to lead, we seek unity for the people of God by proper shepherding. Bringing together various factions and fiefdoms is difficult territory, but there is advice here in the Scriptures as to how it can be achieved.

Pity and sorrow

As we have seen from 2 Samuel 1, the first lesson of unification is through pity, care, and godly sorrow. David writes and sings a song of lament. God uses people who groan for better days, not gloat over mistakes that others have made. The Lord Jesus said, "Blessed are they that mourn" (Matt 5:4).

There are major losses are in every chapter in this transition phase. David mourns each case and does not allow the failures of others to make him hard hearted. It is when we recognise our failure and weakness and believe that God deserves far better than this that blessing comes.

Impartiality and justice

If God's people are going to be united, then leaders will need to be marked by impartiality and to be seen to be doing that which is right and not that which is convenient. The slightest hint of favouritism, and unity becomes impossible. David shows us in these chapters the importance of not only being righteous but modelling righteousness. The Amalekite in 2 Samuel 1 who plundered the dead and thought that David would like the "crown" ended up forfeiting his life. Righteousness must mark David's Kingdom if he was ever to be blessed. He had to make it abundantly clear that he deplored the death of Abner and had nothing to do with it (2 Sam 3). His public act of following on behind the funeral cortege, his sorrow, and his statements in honour of Abner (the man who had put Ishbosheth into power!) and against the "wicked men" resulted in him being seen to be righteous and impartial; "For all the people and all Israel understood that day that it was not of the king to slay Abner the son of Ner" (2 Sam 3:37).

Furthermore, those who killed Ishbosheth, the rival king, in cold blood were themselves killed by David saying: "How much more, when wicked men have slain a righteous person in his own house upon his bed? shall I not therefore now require his blood of your hand, and take you away from the earth?" (2 Sam 4:11). David also ensured that Ishbosheth was given a proper burial (2 Sam 4:12). There was no "club mentality" about David's leadership as he tells us in Psalm 11: "For the righteous LORD loveth righteousness" (Ps 11:7). David would concur with Paul: "Abstain from all appearance of evil" (1 Thess 5:22).

Peace-making

If God's people are going to be united in days of transition, then leaders will need to actively pursue peace. People on all sides of previous divisions need to know that they are loved and that they are accepted. The Lord Jesus said: "Blessed are the peacemakers" (Matt 5:9). The big test for any person is not how they handle their friends but how they handle their enemies. It is not so much their actions that are scrutinised but their reactions. Their instincts and intentions are watched. It not so much the extent of their grace to friends but the extent of their mercy to enemies that results in peace.

David's first act as a new King is not to shower his subjects with gifts but to connect with those who supported his former enemy Saul. In this case it was the people of Jabesh Gilead to whom he actively reached out and praised them for the way they dealt with their master Saul. They had taken his body from the Philistines and buried him (2 Sam 2:4-7). David also acted in a way that put beyond doubt his admiration for Abner calling him a "prince and a great man" (2 Sam 3:38) even although Abner had killed Asahel, one of his mighty men and his cousin (2 Samuel 2).

David made it easy for the two sides (Judah and Ephraim) of Israel to unite. He also made the discussions between both sides transparent. In asking that Michal, his first wife, be brought to him he is showing that "unity" would not be established in a corner in a clandestine fashion but in an open and righteous manner (2 Sam 3). It is interesting that this division between the southern and northern tribes that was healed here, reopened later when David had failed (2 Sam 19:41-43).

David had not tried to kill Saul, Abner or Ishbosheth. Everyone knew he was clear in this matter and had actively sought peace. He had written in Adullam, "... seek peace and pursue it" (Psalm 34:14) and now he was living out his own teaching. The Lord Jesus would teach later: "Love your enemies, bless them that curse you, do good to them that hate you, and pray for them which despitefully use you, and persecute you" (Matt 5:44). David did this. Paul is in keeping with David's philosophy as he stresses the word "you" when he says, "If it be possible, as much as lieth in **you**, live peaceably with all men" (Rom 12:18). So, unity does not come itself - it requires active peace-making even with people who formerly have opposed us: "Be not overcome of evil, but overcome evil with good" (Rom 12:21).

When we observe David's compassionate, just, impartial, peaceable leadership it is no wonder we then read: "Then came all the tribes of Israel to David unto Hebron, and spake, saying, Behold, we are thy bone and thy flesh. Also in time past, when Saul was king over us, thou wast he that leddest out and broughtest in Israel: and the LORD said to thee, Thou shalt feed my people Israel, and thou shalt be a captain over Israel. So all the elders of Israel came to the king to Hebron; and king David made a league with them in Hebron before the LORD: and they anointed David king over Israel" (2 Sam 5:1-3).

Purpose

David's vision as King over all Israel was to establish the royal capital in Jerusalem. We are not sure how the Lord revealed to him that Zion would be "the place which the LORD your God shall choose out of all your tribes to put his name there" (Deut 12:5). He certainly, "perceived that the LORD had established him king over Israel, and that he had exalted his kingdom for his people Israel's sake" (2 Sam 5:12). Nothing seemed to stop him from taking Jerusalem. Strategically, this was a master stroke and pivotal point in the history of Israel and our Bible. Leaders need vison and purpose if they are going to help motivate the people of God. David knew that Hebron was too far south to be the capital and the bridge between the northern and southern territories at Jerusalem seemed ideal to establish the union between the two parts of the country. He clearly was in the mind of God as history bears out. This was an inspired choice: "The LORD loveth the gates of Zion more than all the dwellings of Jacob" (Ps 87:2); "Beautiful for situation, the joy of the whole earth, is mount Zion, on the sides of the north, the city of the great King" (Ps 48:2). In a future day Zechariah would prophesy that Jerusalem will be the capital of the whole Millennial Kingdom: "Sing and rejoice, O daughter of Zion: for, lo, I come, and I will dwell in the midst of thee, saith the LORD. And many nations shall be joined to the LORD in that day, and shall be my people: and I will dwell in the midst of thee, and thou shalt know that the LORD of hosts hath sent me unto thee. And the LORD shall inherit Judah his portion in the holy land, and shall choose Jerusalem again" (Zech 2:10-12). David's vison, therefore, is a classic example of the positive aspect of the Proverb: "Where there is no vision, the people perish" (Prov 29:18).

The choosing of Jerusalem and the binding together of both northern and southern tribes will be accomplished by the Lord Jesus Christ, David's Greater Son, in a coming day: "The envy also of Ephraim shall depart, and the adversaries of Judah shall be cut off: Ephraim shall not envy Judah, and Judah shall not vex Ephraim" (Isa 11:13). And all the world will unite in their praise of Christ as King: "And the LORD shall be king over all the earth: in that day shall there be one LORD, and his name one" (Zech 14:9). David prefigures Christ.

Faith

Jerusalem was one of the finest examples of the art of fortification. It stood on a rocky plateau surrounded on three sides by valleys and was about 11 acres in area, slightly south of the present-day temple-mount site. It could withstand sieges, and the Jebusites who inhabited it bred the arrogance that it could defend itself. This is the meaning of their strange claim that an army of "the blind and lame" could defend it (2 Sam 5:8). However, David had a great God and in faith he took the city. Joab scaled the water course that brought in the city's water supply from the Gihon and showed the Jebusites that their overconfident statement that the city could effectively defend itself was futile. One man with God is a majority.

This vision that David had for Jerusalem as the capital was a vision that Abraham had seen before him as "he looked for a city ... whose builder and maker is God" (Heb 11:10) and was directed to this very mountain – Mount Moriah (Gen 22). Benjamin had tried to take Jerusalem but failed to remove the Jebusites (Judges 1:8, 21). The last of the ten nations whose territory Abram's descendants were to occupy were the Jebusites in the list of Genesis 15:18-21. Now at length the Jebusites are being removed from their citadel and the vison would be realised by David. Soon the Ark will come to Jerusalem (2 Sam 6) and then the threshing floor of Araunah will be shown to be the place of God's House (2 Sam 24). Divine territory is always taken by faith.

Prayer

Full recovery is always found in prayer and in the spirit of dependency. God permits the Philistines to come one final time to test how dear the unity of the whole country is to the heart of David. The Philistines could live with David reigning from Hebron but not over all Israel (2 Sam 5:17). They come to the valley of Rephaim to take the middle ground between Judah and Ephraim so that it would always be two nations with communications being impossible from the North to the South. The Philistines are a picture of the world in the Church. As we have seen in 1 Samuel 17, they came from Egypt, then Cyprus and then to Palestine. They inhabited divine territory but had never crossed the Red Sea or knew anything of redemption. The Philistines did not want unity. They wanted factions and divisions.

David decides to go down to the hold to pray; a wise choice to pray alone to his God. He once again enquires of the Lord whether he should go up against the Philistines and it is affirmed that he should go and smite them (2 Sam 5:19). David obeys and the Philistines are slaughtered. However, after this great victory in prayer and in the battle, the Philistines return. Thankfully, David prays again (v 23). Just after our successes lie our greatest challenges and dangers. Success today can be failure tomorrow. David is learning to move in simple dependence upon God in order to know victory.

Purging of idolatry

After the first victory over the Philistines, David and his men burn the Philistine images (v 21). They had learned that Philistine influence has no place in Zion and so they burned the images to Dagon so that they could never be used again. There is no place for human compromise in the Assembly. The Scriptures require complete separation from all forms of idolatry. Paul would affirm this: "Wherefore, my dearly beloved, flee from idolatry" (1 Cor 10:14); and again: "Wherefore come out from among them, and be ye separate, saith the Lord, and touch not the unclean thing; and I will receive you" (2 Cor 6:17). The removal of all that is offensive to the Lord is the start of real blessing.

Power of God

The Philistines' return does not mean that an identical strategy should be deployed (vv 22-25). David was guided not to repeat the same approach but to come behind the enemy and wait and listen for the "sound of a going in the tops of the mulberry trees". Success would not be in a specific technique but waiting for God to work. David would be conscious of timing in all of his movements. There was no place for human complacency. We, too, must wait in the promptings of the Holy Spirit of God in our movements. The special sense of timing by the Lord Jesus is something we marvel at. Remember the "turn" of the Lord and his "look" over to Peter at just the moment when Peter had denied him three times, as the cock crew! No wonder we read of Peter repenting with bitter tears (Luke 22:61-62). Or we can recall the timing of Philip the evangelist as he drew near to the chariot just as the important verse about the Lord Jesus' death in Isaiah 53 was being read by the Eunuch (Acts 8:30-32). It has often been said if he had waited a few seconds longer he would have found it more difficult to preach "Christ" from Isaiah 54.

David was listening for a sound of wind in the trees. Was he listening to the angelic hosts going out to battle, the feet of angels? "Who layeth the beams of his chambers in the waters: who maketh the clouds his chariot: who walketh upon the wings of the wind: Who maketh his angels spirits; his ministers a flaming fire" (Ps 104:3-4). David was certainly waiting upon God, listening for the still small voice of God, and consequently once again he wrought a great victory. We, too, can know days of triumph as we wait upon God and seek to defend the honour of God from Philistine influence i.e., carnal, worldly people who try to dictate matters in God's House or destroy divine truth. Our success lies in our communion, as we pray to our God and move in simple dependency upon Him, enabled by the Holy Spirit.

PSALM 2

[1] Why do the heathen rage, and the people imagine a vain thing?

[2] The kings of the earth set themselves, and the rulers take counsel together, against the LORD, and against his anointed, saying,

[3] Let us break their bands asunder, and cast away their cords from us.

[4] He that sitteth in the heavens shall laugh: the Lord shall have them in derision.

[5] Then shall he speak unto them in his wrath, and vex them in his sore displeasure.

[6] Yet have I set my king upon my holy hill of Zion.

[7] I will declare the decree: the LORD hath said unto me, Thou art my Son; this day have I begotten thee.

[8] Ask of me, and I shall give thee the heathen for thine inheritance, and the uttermost parts of the earth for thy possession.

[9] Thou shalt break them with a rod of iron; thou shalt dash them in pieces like a potter's vessel.

[10] Be wise now therefore, O ye kings: be instructed, ye judges of the earth.

[11] Serve the LORD with fear, and rejoice with trembling.

[12] Kiss the Son, lest he be angry, and ye perish from the way, when his wrath is kindled but a little. Blessed are all they that put their trust in him.

CHAPTER 12

David: His Convictions

2 Samuel 6-8

This section narrates the high watermark of David's life, with David bringing the Ark of the Covenant back to Jerusalem, and his deep conviction that God should have a House built for His glory. Worship is placed at the heart of the Kingdom. The revelation of the Davidic covenant with the promise of the Kingdom being established for ever is given here. God revealed that he would establish David's household, and the House of God would be built in Jerusalem, initially by David's son. It reminds us of the crucial truth of the House of God and the centrality of God's House in His purposes. All blessing emanates from the House of God. This is also the chapter where David expands the borders of the Kingdom and peace is established with neighbours.

David's convictions about Jerusalem being the place where the Lord had been pleased to place His Name (Deut 12:5) results in him bringing the Ark of the Covenant to Jerusalem. For over 75 years the Ark had not been in the Tabernacle at Shiloh nor was it in the Tabernacle when it moved to Gibeah (2 Chron 1:1-5). The Philistines had captured it (1 Sam 4) before it was returned to Bethshemesh and then taken to the house of Abinadab in Kirjathjearim (1 Sam 5-7). Kirjathjearim is ten miles northwest of Jerusalem. Eventually, the Tabernacle was moved completely into the temple in the reign of Solomon (1 Kings 8:1-4; 2 Chron 5:1-5).

Singularity of God's House

David believed in the singularity of God's House. There was one Ark of the Covenant, not two. There was one Tabernacle. He lived in a day when the Tabernacle was in one place and the Ark in another. This was something he was determined to address. It is believed that David writes in Psalm 132 of his experience of realising that the Ark must come to Jerusalem. He pens, "Lo, we heard of it at Ephratah: we found it in the fields of the wood" (v 6). The phrase, "fields of the wood" is the meaning of the place "Kirjathjearim" where the Ark was resting in the house of Abinadab. He writes, "I will not give sleep to mine eyes, or slumber to mine eyelids, Until I find out a place for the LORD, an habitation for the mighty God of Jacob" (vv 4-5). What a spiritual exercise David had, and what convictions he nourished about the place for the Lord. He said, "We will go into his tabernacles: we will worship at his footstool" (v 7). He believed that, when the Ark came, Jerusalem would be the place of the divine presence. His whole life would revolve around that one place. There was a progressive development of this truth in the life of David. He learned the truth of the place in 2 Samuel 5 as his vision for Jerusalem was formed and confirmed. He learned the truth of the person (Ark) and presence of God in 2 Samuel 6. He then learns the truth of permanency in 2 Samuel 7. David had wanted to make a permanent temple and the story of chapter 7 is that God would build a temple, but it would be Solomon who would construct it.

The truth of the singularity of God's House has never changed. God's House today is the local assembly of believers who gather simply into association with the Name of the Lord Jesus (1 Tim 3:15; 1 Peter 4:17). There is one divine presence (Matt 18:20), one pattern (Acts 2:42-43), and one place (1 Cor 11:18, 20). God never intended to have multiple centres of worship in one place.

David calls 30,000 out of Israel to join him in bringing the Ark to Jerusalem (2 Sam 6:1). This day was more important than even the coronation of the King, for here we have one people, one God, one House. He knew that this conviction was the mind of God as he writes, "For the LORD hath chosen Zion; he hath desired it for his habitation. This is my rest for ever: here will I dwell; for I have desired it" (Ps 132:13-14). David's love for God's House appears in Psalm 26 verse 8: "Lord, I have loved the habitation of thy house and the place where thine honour dwelleth", harmonizing with history - "I have set my affection to the house of my God" (1 Chron 29:3).

David inspires Asaph to share the same convictions for the House of God in Jerusalem writing: "Moreover he refused the tabernacle of Joseph, and chose not the tribe of Ephraim: But chose the tribe of Judah, the mount Zion which he loved. And he built his sanctuary like high palaces, like the earth which he hath established for ever" (Ps 78:67-69).

David's affection for the House of God is relevant for us to this day. Some might have argued that David had enough to do in the Kingdom, but he would have maintained that this was the most important thing he would ever do. It was what God wanted. This principle has never changed.

Sovereignty of the House

We learn in 2 Samuel 6 that we can have an exercise to do something for God that is deep and sure, but we can still do it in the wrong way. The way we do things is important. David brought the Ark to Jerusalem on a new cart (v 3). However, the Ark was never meant to be placed on a cart - it had rings and staves and was designed to be carried. Elaborate details are given to us in Numbers chapter 4 about how the Ark and other holy vessels were to be draped in certain coverings and carried in a sanctified manner. There may have been some logic that it would have been more expeditious to place it on a cart. David would soon learn that there is no place for "human philosophy" in God's House - only the need for simple obedience. The cart was a labour-saving device, and much more efficient, but it had no Scripture to support its use. There may be ways to propagate the Word of God that are more popular, and may make a lot of sense like drama, art, or music, but they all have this in common that there is no scriptural sanction for our use of these methods. The message to us is, "Preach the word" (2 Tim 4:2). In 2 Samuel 6 large crowds accompanied the cart and much music was played (vv 4-5) but, although the crowd approved, God did not. No amount of unity or enthusiasm can compensate for disobedience.

The story of the oxen stumbling, the Ark being jostled, Uzzah stretching out his hand to steady the Ark and being struck down is solemn for all of us (vv 6-8). There needs to be reverence when handling divine matters, and it is a startling reminder about the need for total obedience to the commands of God. The "hand of man" intruding into holy matters is a great grief to God. We must learn the lesson of the divine intolerance of all this. The Ark was not to be dragged or jostled by animals, or touched by human hands. It had to be carried with dignity. We must beware how we speak of the Lord and how we speak to God. There is a fittingness about things. Sometimes people are just untaught, sometimes they have not seen the significance of issues. But if we have been taught the truth of the holiness of God's House then the least that the Lord can expect is for us to obey Him and reverence Him. We will be very careful how we conduct ourselves in His presence in decorum, dress, and dignity, and weigh carefully what we say about our Lord's birth, divinity and death – all are unique. We also need to strive against bringing business-like organising powers into His House.

The New Testament equivalent of Uzzah is the assembly at Corinth where God in His sovereign governance acted directly on the company for treating the sacredness of the Breaking of Bread and regarding it as a common meal. As a result, some were sick, and others had died (1 Cor 11:30-32). The Lord Jesus is still sovereign in His House.

Saints and strangers in the House

After the dreadful scene at Perezuzzah the Ark is taken into the house of Obed-edom the Gittite for three months (vv 11-12). It would not just be any home that could take the Ark of the Covenant. It would have to be a home that was marked by sanctity and a deep sense of reverential awe of God. This home, somewhat surprisingly, belonged to a Gittite, that means a resident of Gath, a Philistine. The Lord blessed this home (v 12), and everyone associated with Obed-edom's house. It is a reminder that God's intentions have always been to bring in Gentiles into the blessing. Even after the Ark is brought from Obed-edom's house to Jerusalem, he is given an important role in the "tent" at Jerusalem: "And Shebaniah, and Jehoshaphat, and Nethaneel, and Amasai, and Zechariah, and Benaiah, and Eliezer, the priests, did blow with the trumpets before the ark of God: and Obed-edom and Jehiah were doorkeepers for the ark" (1 Chron 15:24). Obed-edom saw "sanctification" not as a theoretical thing, but he lived it out. One of the names given to believers is "saints" (1 Cor 1:2); that means we are set apart for God. The character we display and the conditions we uphold are the all-important principles for service in God's House, and not so much our so-called pedigree. We are all simply sinners saved by grace.

Obed-edom had sincerity and was not marked by self-importance or pride. This is why he can be used as a role model for others to live godly lives. All leaders in assembly life should emulate this. Obed-edom was a stranger in Israel and yet had been influenced by David and had come to worship the true God. He pictures a principle of God blessing the Gentile though the Jew as well as God blessing the Jew through the Gentile. It is also reminding us that there is now complete equality between Jews and Gentiles in the Church which is His Body. This key doctrine is put in its fullest form in the Ephesian epistle: "Wherefore remember, that ye being in time past Gentiles in the flesh, who are called Uncircumcision by that which is called the Circumcision in the flesh made by hands; That at that time ye were without Christ, being aliens from the commonwealth of Israel, and strangers from the covenants of promise, having no hope, and without God in the world: But now in Christ Jesus ye who sometimes were far off are made nigh by the blood of Christ" (Eph 2:11-13). There is no distinction in the assembly ethnically, and we can say like Paul: "Now therefore ye are no more strangers and foreigners, but fellow-citizens with the saints, and of the household of God" (Eph 2:19). All of us have equal right to be there.

Obed-edom stayed small – just a door keeper (1 Chron 15:24). So let us learn to take the low place. The Assembly of God is full of different types of people, personalities, ethnic groups and skills. Yet the Assembly is one large choir, where each voice is needed to "shew forth the praises of him who hath called you out of darkness into his marvellous light" (1 Peter 2:9).

Sacrifice and spirit of joy in the House

The Ark is taken into Jerusalem from the house of Obed-edom with great joy (vv 13-19). The lessons have all been learned. The Ark is carried with dignity. There is no hurry or desire to use a cart, indeed every six steps they sacrifice to God. There is no place for shortcuts when it comes to sacrifice. David is bringing up the Ark with great joy (1 Chron 15:25) and the sound of the trumpet. Although there is no Scripture for musical accompaniment in the New Testament there is still no place for staidness or stagnancy in worship. Worship should be warm and have real spiritual energy.

The fact that there was sacrifice every six steps is interesting. It is not seven steps, as our worship always falls short of perfection. But six is the number of divine reflection and representation. On the sixth day God made "man in our image and after our likeness" (Gen 1:26). The number of man is 666 which is the counterfeit image by Satan (Rev 13:18). Satan will always have his counterfeit, but God's original plan was that man might reflect His glory, and His purpose in Christ is that believers might be "conformed to the image of his Son" (Rom 8:29). John exclaims, "... we shall be like him" (1 John 3:2). The space in Ezekiel's temple into the Holiest of All is six cubits (Ezek 41:1-3), and Ruth came back from Boaz with six measures of barley (Ruth 3:15). Therefore, "six" reminds us of divine reflection. We are never more God-like than when we worship: "By him therefore let us offer the sacrifice of praise to God continually, that is, the fruit of our lips giving thanks to his name" (Heb 13:15).

The closeness between the tent where the Ark and the priest were, and the palace where the King lived is interesting. David danced with a linen ephod and also wore royal robe underneath (1 Chron 15:27). He was a saint and a sovereign, a picture of the coming King-Priest in our Lord Jesus.

These great facts were not appreciated by Michal, David's wife

(2 Sam 6:20-23). She did not like David's spiritual exuberance. Our appreciation of Christ and our joy in worship and priesthood will not be appreciated by the carnal. It is good when husbands and wives share the same spiritual interest. This episode reminds us of the difficulties David faced in his marriage to Saul's daughter, and her statement, although not completely lacking in justification, was laced with sarcasm and exposed her lack of conviction about God's House. David was too hasty to marry her in 1 Samuel 18 under Saul's pressure and was paying the consequences of this decision.

Scripture and the House

David had a burden to build a House for God. He wanted a permanent structure to be erected: "See now, I dwell in an house of cedar, but the ark of God dwelleth within curtains" (2 Sam 7:2). He wanted to ensure that God was behind this burden and so he enquired of Nathan the prophet. Nathan was with David in the days of his reigning just as closely as Gad was in the days of his exile. He was with him at this most important moment, as he will be in the dark days of Bathsheba, and in the coronation of Solomon. Initially he is impressed with David's exercise to build a House for God (vv 1-3).

Two commendable features mark Nathan. He is not someone who has the problem of pride: it does not matter to him that this idea did not originate with him, and he encourages David. He also is someone who can admit that they have made a mistake; he initially thought that David should build the House, but later admits he was wrong. God showed him he was too rash to advise David to build a House, instead He explains to him that God would build David a house, and that David's son Solomon would build the House of the Lord. David kept this conviction all his life, purchasing the threshing floor of Ornan the Jebusite (2 Sam 24) and preparing all the materials for Solomon (1 Chron 22:5, 14; 26:27; 29:2-5, 14). It is good when we recognise that others are called to a work and that we are happy to do everything in our power to support them.

David even received the plans from God for the House of God: "All this, said David, the LORD made me understand in writing by his hand upon me, even all the works of this pattern" (1 Chron 28:19). He was learning that God's House is divinely built and that there is a need for revelation of His plan. Nathan speaks of God's plans for His House: "Moreover I will appoint a place for my people Israel, and will plant them" (2 Sam 7:10). The "planting" reminds us of the first garden that the LORD God planted (Gen 2:8), and how the assembly is described as "His garden" (1 Cor 3:9). God established the seven churches in Asia (Rev 2-3), setting each golden lampstand on its own base. God is the owner of the assembly.

David had to appreciate that God's House must be built in God's way and in God's time. David would learn that he would not be the one to build the house, but that he could prepare for it. His own role in relation to the House was very clearly prescribed. We have the revelation in the Scriptures about what we should do today. We are all "labourers together with God" (1 Cor 3:9) and, in accepting the various roles, we are "Endeavouring to keep the unity of the spirit in the bond of peace" (Eph 4:3).

God establishes a covenant with David's house promising that David's seed would be blessed eternally and that from his loins would spring the Messiah and an eternal Kingdom: "thy throne shall be established for ever" (2 Sam 7:16, c.f. v 19). David feels that he is an undeserving case to receive such a covenant saying: "Who am I, O Lord GOD? and what is my house, that thou hast brought me hitherto?" (2 Sam 7:18). He recognised that the Lord knew everything about him and is amazed that he is chosen to do this, "for thou, Lord GOD, knowest thy servant" (2 Sam 7:20). David also recognises that this covenant is unprecedented among the nations: "And what one nation in the earth is like thy people, even like Israel" (2 Sam 7:23). He seems to be consumed with the revelation from God: "For thy word's sake, and according to thine own heart, hast thou done all these great things, to make thy servant know them. Wherefore thou art great, O LORD God ... according to all that we have heard with our ears" (2 Sam 7:21-22). David continues, "thou hast confirmed" (v 24); "thou hast spoken" (v 25); "thou ... hast revealed" (v 27); and "thou hast promised" (v 28). David is simply astonished at what God has revealed to him.

One of the greatest revelations given to us is God's revelation for His House. His Word should be the governing and guiding basis for all activity in His House. Our blueprint is the Bible.

Salvation from the House

It is fascinating that 2 Samuel 8 is to do with the expansion of the borders of Israel. After the Ark is established and God's mind has been made clear in relation to His House in chapter 7, we then read of the victory in war with enemies in eight different countries. This is always God's way. Worship before warfare, prayer before preaching. Feeling our vulnerability in His presence fits us for boldness in testimony in the world. After the ten-day prayer meeting and the worship at Pentecost it was then that Peter preached and 3,000 were saved (Acts 2).

The church in Philadelphia felt their weakness: "for thou hast a little strength". And yet to this church God said: "I have set before thee an open door, and no man can shut it: for thou hast a little strength, and hast kept my word, and hast not denied my name" (Rev 3:8). The whole of the Phrygian plain lay before them for evangelism, and this small assembly rose to this challenge, feeling their inadequacy but confident in their God. Like the assembly in Thessalonica, they became known for their evangelism (1 Thess 1:8). So will every assembly that, feeling their weakness, preach the Word, having put the honour of His House first and ensuring that the Scriptures govern all practice.

PSALM 132

[A Song of degrees.]

¹ LORD, remember David, and all his afflictions:

² How he sware unto the LORD, and vowed unto the mighty God of Jacob;

³ Surely I will not come into the tabernacle of my house, nor go up into my bed;

⁴ I will not give sleep to mine eyes, or slumber to mine eyelids,

⁵ Until I find out a place for the LORD, an habitation for the mighty God of Jacob.

⁶ Lo, we heard of it at Ephratah: we found it in the fields of the wood.

⁷ We will go into his tabernacles: we will worship at his footstool.

⁸ Arise, O LORD, into thy rest; thou, and the ark of thy strength.

⁹ Let thy priests be clothed with righteousness; and let thy saints shout for joy.

¹⁰ For thy servant David's sake turn not away the face of thine anointed.

¹¹ The LORD hath sworn in truth unto David; he will not turn from it; Of the fruit of thy body will I set upon thy throne.

¹² If thy children will keep my covenant and my testimony

that I shall teach them, their children shall also sit upon thy throne for evermore.

¹³ For the LORD hath chosen Zion; he hath desired it for his habitation.

¹⁴ This is my rest for ever: here will I dwell; for I have desired it.

¹⁵ I will abundantly bless her provision: I will satisfy her poor with bread.

¹⁶ I will also clothe her priests with salvation: and her saints shall shout aloud for joy.

¹⁷ There will I make the horn of David to bud: I have ordained a lamp for mine anointed.

¹⁸ His enemies will I clothe with shame: but upon himself shall his crown flourish.

PSALM 60

[To the chief Musician upon Shushaneduth, Michtam of David, to teach; when he strove with Aramnaharaim and with Aramzobah, when Joab returned, and smote of Edom in the valley of salt twelve thousand.]

¹ O God, thou hast cast us off, thou hast scattered us, thou hast been displeased; O turn thyself to us again.

² Thou hast made the earth to tremble; thou hast broken it: heal the breaches thereof; for it shaketh.

³ Thou hast shewed thy people hard things: thou hast made us to drink the wine of astonishment.

⁴ Thou hast given a banner to them that fear thee, that it may be displayed because of the truth. Selah.

⁵ That thy beloved may be delivered; save with thy right hand, and hear me.

⁶ God hath spoken in his holiness; I will rejoice, I will divide Shechem, and mete out the valley of Succoth.

⁷ Gilead is mine, and Manasseh is mine; Ephraim also is the strength of mine head; Judah is my lawgiver;

⁸ Moab is my washpot; over Edom will I cast out my shoe: Philistia, triumph thou because of me.

⁹ Who will bring me into the strong city? who will lead me into Edom?

¹⁰ Wilt not thou, O God, which hadst cast us off? and thou, O God, which didst not go out with our armies?11 Give us help from trouble: for vain is the help of man.

¹² Through God we shall do valiantly: for he it is that shall tread down our enemies.

CHAPTER 13

David: His Compassion

2 Samuel 9-10

David is now settled in the Kingdom and his mind turns to those to whom he would like to show kindness. His choices illustrate his compassion and generous disposition. In 2 Samuel 9 he will show kindness to the offspring of King Saul, his former enemy, and in 2 Samuel 10 he will show kindness to Hanun the new king of Ammon, a group that had plagued God's people (c.f. Jepthah in Judges 10-12 and Saul in 1 Samuel 11). In 2 Samuel 9 the kindness is surprising, and in 2 Samuel 10 the kindness is spurned as Hanun ridicules David's men who came to show sympathy at the time of his (Hanun's) father's death. This section provides important lessons about compassion and benevolence, and how we react when this is rejected.

Chapter 9   Mephibosheth – Unexpected Kindness

The kindness of David

David enquires after the progeny of Jonathan: "Is there yet any that is left of the house of Saul, that I may shew him kindness for Jonathan's sake?" (2 Sam 9:1). He learns of one, Mephibosheth, who had been incapacitated in his legs after being dropped as a child of five years by his nurse when news came that his father Jonathan and his grandfather Saul had died (2 Sam 4:4). David sought to bless Saul's seed despite Saul's ill treatment towards him, and showered blessings on Mephibosheth who ate at David's table every day as one of his sons (2 Sam 9: 7, 11, 13).

It is a lovely picture of the grace of our Lord Jesus Christ to sinners such as ourselves: Through Christ, "the kindness and love of God our Saviour toward man appeared" (Titus 3:4). And just as David's kindness to Mephibosheth was not a one-off, Paul looks ahead for the believers in Christ and exclaims: "That in the ages to come he might shew the exceeding riches of his grace in his kindness toward us through Christ Jesus" (Eph 2:7).

How far does our compassion and kindness extend? Certainly, the early church fed and sheltered daily those widows who had no-one to help them (Acts 6; 1 Timothy 5), and Dorcas made clothes for the poor in Acts 9:36. The Lord's teaching to us is as clear as it is difficult to attain: "Then said he also to him that bade him, When thou makest a dinner or a supper, call not thy friends, nor thy brethren, neither thy kinsmen, nor thy rich neighbours; lest they also bid thee again, and a recompence be made thee. But when thou makest a feast, call the poor, the maimed, the lame, the blind: And thou shalt be blessed; for they cannot recompense thee: for thou shalt be recompensed at the resurrection of the just" (Luke 14:12-14). The Assembly of God should be marked by care, and ought to be the most inclusive place in the world.

The wisdom of David

Mephibosheth was not made to feel like he was a "charity case" or an "invalid" who had no personal authority but would live off David's kindness. Instead, all the land previously owned by Saul was given to him (v 7). Mephibosheth took full authority for this estate and employed Ziba (Saul's servant) and his family to look after the land for him (v 10). The ability to show kindness requires real diplomacy. It is not just about giving; it is about how we give.

The truth of David

David had promised Jonathan with a covenant that he would bless his seed after the Lord had "cut off the enemies of David" (1 Sam 20:14-17; 42). This was initiated in 1 Samuel 18:3, confirmed in 20:16, and reiterated in 23:16-18. David never forgot his promise and was true to his word. He did this despite no one else knowing about his covenant promise. But God knew about it, and David was a man of his word. God blesses honesty. David also kept his word not out of a slavish sense of duty but from genuine love for Jonathan.

The encouragement of David

David said, "Fear not" to Mephibosheth (v 7). Mephibosheth would have heard many negative things about David from his grandfather Saul, and possibly Ishbosheth, and would have been deeply suspicious of what was happening. David did not try to sit him down and set the record straight. However, the way in which David handled Mephibosheth blew all negative thoughts from his mind. The warmth of David would have shown Mephibosheth that his apprehension and prejudices were ill founded. We all need to be aware of this. We can build very wrong thoughts about people in our minds.

Instead of being afraid, Mephibosheth was taken up with God's goodness to him as a completely undeserving case. He recognised there was no merit in himself, describing himself a "dead dog" (v 8), i.e., less than a servant. It was for "Jonathan's sake" he was blessed. We too have no merit in ourselves. Like Mephibosheth, we have no right to be made one of the sons of God (Gal 3:26). We are simply sinners saved by grace and blessed for our Lord Jesus Christ's sake (Eph 4:32). Mephibosheth's love for the King is remarkable, and in 19:30 he wants nothing else but David, calling him "my lord the king". True worship rises above even our blessings to the Blesser himself.

The leadership of David

Most kings of that era would have destroyed the seed of the previous king to prevent any rival rising to usurp the throne - David did the opposite. Most kings of that era would also have destroyed the lands of the previous king - David granted it to Saul's seed and appointed Saul's servants to administer it. Mephibosheth had been a casualty of war, having been crippled when Saul was killed in Gilboa, and at an early age saw his uncle Ishbosheth killed in cold blood. David did everything in his power to "restore" (v 7) the situation. Many brothers and sisters have been damaged by the wars of others and they need help. But David understood that better days were ahead and firmly believed that Mephibosheth did not need to be defined by his past. David also saw another generation rising in Mephibosheth's son Micha (v 12) and had the vision to believe that those seared in the past can be healed and rise to usefulness in the Kingdom. We need leaders today with a similar vision.

The Christlikeness of David

David was a man after God's own heart (1 Sam 13:14; Acts 13:22), and his love for Mephibosheth surely illustrates this. David made the first move towards Mephibosheth just as our blessed Lord did for us in the day of our weakness and sin (Rom 5:8; 1 John 4:19). Mephibosheth felt like a "dead dog" (v 8) and we too, as believers in Christ, were "dead in trespasses and sins" but the Lord Jesus Christ has given us new life (Eph 2:1-6). David did not need to go so far to keep his promise to Jonathan, but in grace and love he went beyond the call of duty. Similarly our blessed Lord goes beyond law: "the law was given by Moses but grace and truth came by Jesus Christ" (John 1:17) It says four times that Mephibosheth will eat at David's table (vv 7, 10, 11, 13), and we too are taught that God "raised us up together, and made us sit together in heavenly places in Christ Jesus: That in the ages to come he might shew the exceeding riches of his grace in his kindness toward us through Christ Jesus" (Eph 2:6-7).

The blessing upon David

David's kindness to the crippled son of Jonathan would not go unnoticed by the Lord. Mephibosheth was loyal to David even when Absalom usurped his father, and Mephibosheth's servant Ziba slandered him. While David was at his lowest Mephibosheth stood by him and wanted nothing in return (2 Sam 19:24-30). When we show kindness to others, looking for nothing in return, this often results in kindness being repaid at the time of our greatest need: "He that hath pity upon the poor lendeth unto the LORD; and that which he hath given will he pay him again" (Prov 19:17).

Chapter 10   Hanun – Rejected Kindness

David loves his enemies

Chapters nine and ten of 2 Samuel sit side by side for a reason. In chapter 9 David is showing kindness to a disinherited, disabled grandson of King Saul, David's enemy. In chapter 10, David shows kindness to Hanun the king of Ammon who had been appointed king after the death of his father Nahash. The Ammonites, although distant cousins of Israel being the offspring of Lot (Gen 19:38), were often attacking God's people (Judges 10-12). King Saul destroyed the Ammonites after they intended to take the right eye of the residents of Jabesh Gilead, and a result of his victory he was anointed King in Gilgal (1 Sam 11:15). Nevertheless, David showed pity, reminding us of the Lord's teaching: "But I say unto you, Love your enemies, bless them that curse you, do good to them that hate you, and pray for them which despitefully use you, and persecute you" (Matt 5:44).

David remembers the faithfulness of others

Normally kings destroy all rival enemies, but David was different. He knew that the children of Lot (including Ammon) had been given their land by God (Deut 2:19). He also had been on peaceful terms with Hanun's father Nahash, and it is implied within the word "kindness" that there was a covenant promise that he would look after his seed. David said, "I will shew kindness unto Hanun the son of Nahash, as his father shewed kindness unto me" (v 2). It may be that this friendship was cemented when David was being pursued by Saul, or when David was at Ziklag. Either way, David is determined to comfort Hanun at the death of his father, and assure him of his support by sending an embassage. David certainly did not forget previous kindness. Hanun would have done well to remember the Proverb: "Thine own friend, and thy father's friend, forsake not" (Prov 27:10).

David's motive is questioned

Hanun's court officials are suspicious of this kindness, and question David's motive for sending the ambassadors to sympathise (v 3). Rehoboam took false advice from his courtiers, and it divided the Kingdom (1 Kings 12:13-16). We need to be very careful who we listen to. False men are apt to think that others are as false as they are. Some people believe that their neighbours could never have any good will towards them simply because they themselves could never have good will towards their neighbours. Love ... "thinketh no evil" (1 Cor 13:5). Let us stand apart from this type of behaviour and, without being gullible, give people the benefit of the doubt. We ought to look for the best in others and not speculate about false motives for good actions. This is the meaning of the Lord's teaching, "Judge not, and ye shall not be judged: condemn not, and ye shall not be condemned". He is not speaking of not judging sin but He is condemning a hyper-critical and suspicious spirit. The Lord taught instead: "Give, and it shall be given unto you; good measure, pressed down, and shaken together, and running over, shall men give into your bosom. For with the same measure that ye mete withal it shall be measured to you again" (Luke 6:37-38).

The court officials go further and allege that David wants to overthrow the Ammonites, saying that the ambassadors are spies, and scurrilously suggest that all this "sympathy" is simply a scouting mission prior to a full scale invasion (v 3). This gives licence for ruthless and insulting behaviour to David's servants – shaving off half their beards (which in that culture was considered disgraceful, Lev 19:27) and cutting their clothes off just above their buttocks, which was tantamount to making them prisoners of war (Isa 20:3-4). They were then sent back to Israel in this state "greatly ashamed" (vv 4-5). Whatever the international code was for dealing with diplomats at that time, it was broken by Hanun!

David's wise counsel to wait

This episode in David's life has instruction for us when our kindness is rejected. When David hears of the shameful way his emissaries have been dealt with, he tells them to stay at Jericho until their beards are grown (v 5). Take time to wait upon God is David's response. This "space" to reflect and pray would have been more than a few days. But tempers can cool, beards can grow back, clothes can be acquired, and the unjust reproach will wear off, but what remains is the shame on the perpetrators and the stain on their character. We need calm heads when we have been wronged and remember that those who have wronged us are the ones who have lost the most. It is a wonderful thing to be able to have clear blue sky between ourselves and God and know that we have not done anything that would have brought Him shame. We need patience: "wait, I say, on the Lord" (Ps 27:14). "Beloved, if our heart condemn us not, then have we confidence toward God. And whatsoever we ask, we receive of him, because we keep his commandments, and do those things that are pleasing in his sight" (1 John 3:21-22).

David is aware of the weakness of his brethren

David also asked the men to stay in Jericho. He did not want everyone at the palace in Jerusalem to know what had happened. If he had reacted badly than there would have been those around David who might have started a war! We need to be aware of the weaknesses of others. People can be so angry at the way their leaders are treated that they take matters into their own hands. Leaders must remember that their actions are not neutral, and they can influence people by their response. Unlike Nabal, David does not rush in but encourages his ambassadors to delay their return and let their beards grow. The men of Zeruiah would have killed Saul in the cave (1 Sam 24), or with Saul's spear in Ziph (1 Sam 26), or slain Shimei after the victory over Absalom (2 Sam 19:21-22), but David had learned patience. David had appreciated through Abigail the danger of rushing in too quickly: "Some men's sins are open beforehand, going before to judgment; and some men they follow after" (1 Tim 5:24). Let us be slow to react and be aware of the weaknesses in others.

David is forced to defend divine territory

Interestingly, it is Ammon who comes against David with a huge army, swollen by the hired forces of Syria (v 6). Often the party which are the cause of the problem make the first move – "He that is first in his own cause seemeth just; but his neighbour cometh and searcheth him" (Prov 18:17). Ultimately, David is forced to go into the battle himself, and in God's strength through Joab's skill he routs the Ammonites (vv 7-14), and then he personally leads the army of Israel to victory against the Syrians (vv 15-19) after Joab had besieged Rabbah, the capital of the Ammonite lands (1 Chron 19:17-19). Sometimes we simply must defend divine territory. Ultimately the Ammonites "made peace" and "served them [Israel]" (v 19). God will always bless righteous behaviour.

Lessons for today

When we reach out in kindness this is not always accepted. Ever remember, if we find ourselves in this situation, that the kindness of our Lord Jesus was rejected and they placed Him, the Lord of glory, on a cross. We, too, must look after those affected by the insults of others. We need patience and time to wait upon the Lord and do nothing to stir up the emotions of those close to us. God will be the judge, and we must rely upon Him to defend divine truth. Be ready to be used to defend the truth of God, but never work on the principle of retaliation when kindness is refused. Let the Apostle Paul have the last word: "And be ye kind one to another, tenderhearted, forgiving one another, even as God for Christ's sake hath forgiven you" (Eph 4:32).

PSALM 103

[A Psalm of David.]

¹ Bless the LORD, O my soul: and all that is within me, bless his holy name.

² Bless the LORD, O my soul, and forget not all his benefits:

³ Who forgiveth all thine iniquities; who healeth all thy diseases;

⁴ Who redeemeth thy life from destruction; who crowneth thee with lovingkindness and tender mercies;

⁵ Who satisfieth thy mouth with good things; so that thy youth is renewed like the eagle's.

⁶ The LORD executeth righteousness and judgment for all that are oppressed.

⁷ He made known his ways unto Moses, his acts unto the children of Israel.

⁸ The LORD is merciful and gracious, slow to anger, and plenteous in mercy.

⁹ He will not always chide: neither will he keep his anger for ever.

¹⁰ He hath not dealt with us after our sins; nor rewarded us according to our iniquities.

¹¹ For as the heaven is high above the earth, so great is his mercy toward them that fear him.

¹² As far as the east is from the west, so far hath he removed our transgressions from us.

¹³ Like as a father pitieth his children, so the LORD pitieth them that fear him.

14 For he knoweth our frame; he remembereth that we are dust.

15 As for man, his days are as grass: as a flower of the field, so he flourisheth.

16 For the wind passeth over it, and it is gone; and the place thereof shall know it no more.

17 But the mercy of the LORD is from everlasting to everlasting upon them that fear him, and his righteousness unto children's children;

18 To such as keep his covenant, and to those that remember his commandments to do them.

19 The LORD hath prepared his throne in the heavens; and his kingdom ruleth over all.

20 Bless the LORD, ye his angels, that excel in strength, that do his commandments, hearkening unto the voice of his word.

21 Bless ye the LORD, all ye his hosts; ye ministers of his, that do his pleasure.

22 Bless the LORD, all his works in all places of his dominion: bless the LORD, O my soul.

CHAPTER 14

David: His Collapse

2 Samuel 11-13

These chapters deal with a terribly sad event in the life of David. David fails morally with Bathsheba and the repercussions are awful, moving from initial attraction to adultery to the murder of Uriah, Bathsheba's husband. The prophet Nathan is forced to tell him in no uncertain terms, "Thou art the man", and that God would avenge him fourfold. Around this point of time, two of David's sons die - the child born to Bathsheba, and his son Ammon who is killed by another of his sons, Absalom. The death of Absalom and his fourth son Adonijah will follow in subsequent chapters. This section details how we can avoid falling into the same error, how sin leaves its impact but also provides hope in that forgiveness and restoration can be found with the Lord.

David's cataclysmic failure and subsequent "cover-up" sins make for harrowing reading resulting in collateral damage to the throne and the family. The parallels between chapters 11-12 and chapter 13 are too obvious to miss. In chapters 11-12 the subject matters are the adultery between David and Bathsheba and the murder of Uriah, and in chapter 13 the subject matters are rape by Amnon of his sister Tamar and the murder of Amnon by Absalom his brother in an act of revenge. We learn, therefore, several things about moral failure in this dreadful episode in the life of David.

The Bible does not hide these sins, so that we might learn from the mistakes of the past. David's failure underscores our own vulnerability. If someone as great as David could fail, then let us heed Paul's warning: "Let him that thinketh he standeth take heed lest he fall" (1 Cor 10:12). Generations later, the testimony of David by the Spirit of God was, "David did that which was right in the eyes of the

LORD, and turned not aside from any thing that he commanded him all the days of his life, save only in the matter of Uriah the Hittite" (1 Kings 15:5). David did live for God, but this awful blemish on David's testimony is recorded for us in full detail along with his prayer of repentance (Psalm 51), so that we can take avoiding action.

Apathy

The danger of being idle is brought forcibly to us in this sad chapter of David's life. After the destruction of the Syrians (2 Sam 10) who the Ammonites had hired to kill David, he then turns his mind to dealing with Ammonites and their capital city of Rabbah, the centre of the insurrection. This time, however, he does not go himself but sends Joab to besiege Rabbah (2 Sam 11:1). David is waiting on word from Joab for the point where the siege would be over, and then he intended to take the city. He anticipates joining them then, which he does later as recorded for us in 2 Samuel 12:26-31. It is during this period of idleness that the dreadful deed takes place. It is when he has too much leisure time on the roof of his house that he sins. The adage is true "The devil finds work for idle hands to do". We need to keep busy. We need to keep thinking of others. David should have been soldiering with his brethren not sleeping! Peter and Paul warn us to waken up: "Be sober, be vigilant; because your adversary the devil, as a roaring lion, walketh about, seeking whom he may devour" (1 Peter 5:8); "Therefore let us not sleep, as do others; but let us watch and be sober. For they that sleep sleep in the night; and they that be drunken are drunken in the night. But let us, who are of the day, be sober, putting on the breastplate of faith and love; and for an helmet, the hope of salvation" (1 Thess 5:6-8). Therefore, let us be alert and on our guard and fill our time with purposeful, spiritual activity.

Indiscretion

From the height of the palace roof David sees Bathsheba bathing (v 2). Whether Bathsheba was being deliberately immodest or not we do not know, but she was certainly being indiscreet. We cannot be too careful when it comes to clothing and what we reveal about our bodies. The world is besotted with worshipping the body and flaunting it. Peter says we are altogether different: "But let it be the hidden man of the heart, in that which is not corruptible, even the ornament of a meek and quiet spirit, which is in the sight of God of great price" (1 Peter 3:4). Let us be careful what we wear in public and how we conduct ourselves in the sight of others. It does not take much to start a chain of sin. "But put ye on the Lord Jesus Christ, and make not provision for the flesh, to fulfil the lusts thereof" (Rom 13:14).

The lustful eye

We do not know what our eye is going to see but we do not need to prolong the moment. "Flee fornication", is the teaching of Scripture (1 Cor 6:18). Joseph learned to flee from the advances of the wife of Potiphar (Gen 39:12), and the Lord taught us that looking upon a woman to lust is adultery (Matt 5:28). David should not have been on the roof when his brethren were warring, and he certainly should have got off the roof when he saw Bathsheba exposing herself. Give the flesh no room to manoeuvre. If we feed the flesh it will grow. Peter warns: "Dearly beloved, I beseech you as strangers and pilgrims, abstain from fleshly lusts, which war against the soul" (1 Peter 2:11). David did not know how costly the prolonging of this sinful moment would become.

Prolonging the problem

David, most unwisely, goes on to find out more about Bathsheba. If we continue to think about something it can become a fetish and an uncontrollable urge. These things need to be nipped in the bud quickly. Even when David discovers Bathsheba is married it does not seem to deter him. Is this why the Lord asks us to cut out our eye if our eye is being focused on sinful things lest both eyes be cast into hell (Matt 5:28-29)? He is not speaking of self-harm, but, by use of hyperbole, is making clear the drastic steps we need to take to keep ourselves pure or we will suffer eternal consequences. For some this may mean having to move house to get away from godless people, for others it might be avoiding certain places, or evading certain people or things, while for yet others it might mean stopping all social media and even living without the internet. We must take active steps to stop ourselves thinking and acting in this way. This will require the power of the Holy Spirit, and in His power, it is possible to do so. The Scriptures assure us of this: "This I say then, Walk in the Spirit, and ye shall not fulfil the lust of the flesh" (Gal 5:16). So, there is a clear promise of victory if we "Walk in the Spirit".

The act of sin

David sends messengers to bring Bathsheba to him and commits adultery with her (v 4). He was responsible, for he was in a very commanding and controlling position as King. It is possible that Bathsheba felt she had to comply. Adultery is a breach of the seventh commandment (Ex 20:14) and is condemned in the New Testament: "Now the works of the flesh are manifest, which are these; Adultery, fornication, uncleanness, lasciviousness" (Gal 5:19). The justification of the ceremonial cleansing of Bathsheba from her monthly cycle is ironic (v 4). We can find incredible excuses in our most wicked moments. The speed of the way in which all this happened reminds us how quickly sin can move from the bud into the full bloom. The most unholy thoughts, language and actions can snowball with incredible pace.

The cover up

David learns that Bathsheba is pregnant (v 5). It is taking the verse out of context to quote the phrase, "Be sure your sin will find you out" (Num 32:23) but it seems appropriate here. This fact that Bathsheba is found to be expecting a child seems to send David into a frenzy of foolish behaviour by trying to cover up his sins in going to extraordinary lengths to try to get Uriah (Bathsheba's husband) to lie with his wife to convince him that he would ultimately think he was the father of the child (vv 6-12). Sin leads to further sins and subterfuge. If ever there was a story that highlights the importance of Proverbs 28:13, it is this one: "He that covereth his sins shall not prosper". Uriah, on the other hand, displays an attitude fit for a soldier of the King by remaining loyal and committed to the war on the front line despite David's shocking attempts to encourage him to indulge himself with his wife. Uriah rightly deserves to be thought of when Paul says to Timothy: "Thou therefore endure hardness, as a good soldier of Jesus Christ. No man that warreth entangleth himself with the affairs of this life; that he may please him who hath chosen him to be a soldier" (2 Tim 2:3-4). No wonder David places him on his list of mighty men (2 Sam 23:39), albeit his name comes last. Was David tempted to leave him off, but the Spirit of God forced him to pen Uriah's name?

The escalation to further evil

The ultimate solution of murdering Uriah by proxy (vv 14-25) is a dreadful sorrow which shows how "sin, when it is finished, bringeth forth death" (James 1:15). The idle but innocent look from the roof, which was deliberately prolonged, has resulted in adultery, and now David is a cold-blooded murderer, signing the death warrant and unbelievably sending it by the hand of Uriah to Joab. Sin always starts small but soon swells. "A little leaven leaveneth the whole lump" (1 Cor 5:6). "Behold, how great a matter a little fire kindleth!" (James 3:5). We must learn that when we start to sin, we are not in control of what happens next. The solemn response from the Lord is, "But the thing that David had done displeased the LORD" (v 27). God does not forget.

The man of God

God sends Nathan to reveal to David his sin. This must have happened at least 9 months later as the baby is born already (12:14). We must not assume that, even if we are not immediately judged, God has forgotten. Nor should be assume that sin cannot be successful – up till this point the plan has gone like clockwork. The fact that something appears to work does not make it right. God sometimes allows things to happen to test our obedience. Nathan is the right man to address this matter with David, having been the man David turned to when pondering whether he should build a house for God. Nathan had also been used to tell David of God's covenant with him. It needed the right man to undertake this task. Moral authority was needed. Paul says, "Ye which are spiritual, restore such an one" (Gal 6:1).

The word of God

Nathan uses the parable format to get his message over (12:1-6). Stories can speak louder than words as this tale surely did. The simple description of the rich man with lots of flocks of sheep and herds of cattle, taking and killing the only little lamb of the poor man which he had raised like one of his children, would enrage any hearer. David engages with the story and is indignant, angrily insisting that the rich man should restore the poor man's lamb fourfold. The flesh is capable of condemning loudly the faults of others whilst overlooking our own failures entirely. After David's outburst there come these most chilling words from Nathan the prophet – "Thou art the man" (12:7). These were an arrow to David's soul. Scriptures convict us of sin - they always do.

Repentance

David is immediately faced with the awfulness of his iniquity and descends into a chasm of contrition, learning how hard the road of repentance is, as is recorded for us in Psalm 51. The cries of, "Have mercy upon me, O God", "Wash me", "cleanse me", "Purge me", move us as we read the extent of his sorrow over his sin. The child of Bathsheba sickens and dies. David prayed and fasted all the time the child was sick hoping for the infant to live but believing that, if he died, he would pass straight to glory. David said of his dead child, "But now he is dead, wherefore should I fast? can I bring him back again? I shall go to him, but he shall not return to me". This statement has helped many people whose children have died young. We believe there is provision in the death of Christ for all children. Sometimes they are taken to heaven early to escape the dreadful world down here. This child certainly was.

Ramifications

There are some tokens of blessing as Solomon is born and Rabbah is taken, but the prophecy of restoring "fourfold" did come to pass. The child dies, Amnon is killed by his brother in chapter 13, Absalom himself is slain in chapter 18, and Adonijah will be ultimately killed by Solomon (1 Kings 2). Also, Bathsheba's grandfather Ahithophel (2 Sam 11:3; 23:34) never forgave David for what he did to Bathsheba and Uriah, and he was instrumental in the Absalom rebellion. Joab, who received the letter penned by David that effectively was Uriah's death warrant, was uncontrolled in his behaviour after this point. David did not have the moral authority to challenge him. Amnon fails morally, in the same area as his father, in chapter 13. Sin leaves sorrow. Surely, "the way of transgressors is hard" (Prov 13:15).

Finally, we learn in chapter 12:26-31 of the taking of Rabbah, the royal city of Ammon. This must have happened during the period when David was unrepentant, given the narrative in chapters 10 and 11, and is only recorded here after the whole story with Bathsheba is completed. The ruthless and barbaric behaviour of David to the Ammonites (12:31) speaks of the behaviour of an unrepentant heart. This attitude is so different to the kindness David wanted to show to them in chapter 10. When people are out of sorts with God they lack forgiveness and tenderness.

PSALM 51

[To the chief Musician, A Psalm of David, when Nathan the prophet came unto him, after he had gone in to Bathsheba.]

¹ Have mercy upon me, O God, according to thy lovingkindness: according unto the multitude of thy tender mercies blot out my transgressions.

² Wash me throughly from mine iniquity, and cleanse me from my sin.

³ For I acknowledge my transgressions: and my sin is ever before me.

⁴ Against thee, thee only, have I sinned, and done this evil in thy sight: that thou mightest be justified when thou speakest, and be clear when thou judgest.

⁵ Behold, I was shapen in iniquity; and in sin did my mother conceive me.

⁶ Behold, thou desirest truth in the inward parts: and in the hidden part thou shalt make me to know wisdom.

⁷ Purge me with hyssop, and I shall be clean: wash me, and I shall be whiter than snow.

⁸ Make me to hear joy and gladness; that the bones which thou hast broken may rejoice.

⁹ Hide thy face from my sins, and blot out all mine iniquities.

¹⁰ Create in me a clean heart, O God; and renew a right spirit within me.

¹¹ Cast me not away from thy presence; and take not thy holy spirit from me.

¹² Restore unto me the joy of thy salvation; and uphold me with thy free spirit.

¹³ Then will I teach transgressors thy ways; and sinners shall be converted unto thee.

¹⁴ Deliver me from bloodguiltiness, O God, thou God of my salvation: and my tongue shall sing aloud of thy righteousness.

¹⁵ O Lord, open thou my lips; and my mouth shall shew forth thy praise.

¹⁶ For thou desirest not sacrifice; else would I give it: thou delightest not in burnt offering.

¹⁷ The sacrifices of God are a broken spirit: a broken and a contrite heart, O God, thou wilt not despise.

¹⁸ Do good in thy good pleasure unto Zion: build thou the walls of Jerusalem.

¹⁹ Then shalt thou be pleased with the sacrifices of righteousness, with burnt offering and whole burnt offering: then shall they offer bullocks upon thine altar.

CHAPTER 15

David: His Curse

2 Samuel 14-19a

We now come to a most tragic time in the life of David. His own son, Absalom, ultimately hounds his father off the throne. Chapter 14 commences with a weakened David, after the Bathsheba incident, and he seems unable to deal with Absalom who killed Amnon. Absalom initially runs to Geshur in Arabia (2 Sam 13:38) and stays there in isolation. Joab notes David's inability to bring Absalom back and intervenes using an elaborate ploy commissioning a woman of Tekoa to speak to David about a hypothetical situation in order to convince him to bring Absalom back (2 Sam 14). Joab's underhand approach is an attempt to create a more normalised situation which ultimately convinces David to let Joab bring Absalom back to Jerusalem, although he does not speak to him. The murder of Ammon by Absalom, however, is never dealt with, resulting in Absalom being given opportunity to promote himself and his own ideas. He grows in popularity and arrogance (2 Sam 14:25). After two years at Jerusalem, never seeing David, he ruthlessly burns Joab's field down to demand a meeting with his father, and when he is given an audience, he shows his true character by promoting himself to a place of prominence through flattery with the people (15:1-6). His next step is to directly oppose his own father. By the time we reach chapter 16 he has usurped the throne, sent David into hiding across the Jordan, and callously raped the women of David's court publicly.

Absalom ultimately decides to take the whole country to war against his father David contrary to the counsel of Ahithophel and following Hushai's advice (2 Sam 17). This results in Ahithophel committing suicide for the shame of his counsel not being accepted. Absalom's forces are overcome by David's men and Absalom is finally killed in war after his head was caught in a tree when he was on horseback, and he was then slain by Joab. When King David hears the news, he is deeply affected, crying, "O Absalom my son, my son" (2 Sam 18). Joab severely warns David that perpetuating this behaviour will result in him losing the hearts of the nation, and so he comes to the gate to encourage his people and the process of restoring the Kingdom commences (start of 2 Sam 19).

These chapters, whilst showing us the evil ways of power-hungry wicked men, also illustrate how important friendships are in a time of great trial. There are seven ways in which David is supported during this very trying period. The seven companions of David who helped him at this dreadful time provide lessons to us about how we can help others in a crisis.

Ittai – a warrior (2 Sam 15:17-23)

Ittai was a loyal soldier who said he would be willing to die for David. Some of the most beautiful words of friendship found in Scripture are said by Ittai at this dreadful time in David's life:

"And the king went forth, and all the people after him, and tarried in a place that was far off. And all his servants passed on beside him; and all the Cherethites, and all the Pelethites, and all the Gittites, six hundred men which came after him from Gath, passed on before the king. Then said the king to Ittai the Gittite, Wherefore goest thou also with us? return to thy place, and abide with the king: for thou art a stranger, and also an exile. Whereas thou camest but yesterday, should I this day make thee go up and down with us? seeing I go whither I may, return thou, and take back thy brethren: mercy and truth be with thee. And Ittai answered the king, and said, As the LORD liveth, and as my lord the king liveth, surely in what place my lord the king shall be, whether in death or life, even there also will thy servant be. And David said to Ittai, Go and pass over. And Ittai the Gittite passed over, and all his men, and all the little ones that were with him. And all the country wept with a loud voice, and all the people passed over: the king also himself passed over the brook Kidron, and all the people passed over, toward the way of the wilderness" (2 Sam 15:17-23).

Ittai was a Gittite, from Gath, a Philistine. The men he commanded, the Cherethites (Cherethi – meaning executioners), were a strong tribe closely associated with the Philistines and lived near Ziklag on the south of Judah (1 Sam 30:14). They inhabited the area near the sea and are almost synonymous with the Philistines (Zeph 2:5 c.f. Ezek 25:16). The relationship David forged with them as he protected them from the Amalekites explains their loyalty to him now as King, as it also does that of the Philistines in David's army. The Pelethites are mentioned always along with the Cherethites. The word probably means "runners" or "couriers", and may indicate that, while forming part of David's bodyguard, they were also sometimes employed as couriers (2 Samuel 8:18; 1 Kings 1:38; 1 Kings 1:44; 1 Chronicles 18:17).

Thus, these men that followed Ittai were from a foreign land and yet were filled with love for David. They were brought in by grace. It reminds us of Ruth the Moabitess' words to Boaz: "Why have I found grace in thine eyes, that thou shouldest take knowledge of me, seeing I am a stranger?" (Ruth 2:10). Ittai came to know David in a day of rejection by Saul and saw him crowned "King". His loyalty and allegiance were powerful. He loved David and revelled in the fact that David loved him. He reminds us of a first-generation Christian like John the apostle, who called himself a "disciple whom Jesus loved". Ittai's expression of loyalty, "in what place my lord the king shall be, whether in death or life, even there also will thy servant be", is remarkable and moving. It reminds us of Ruth's statement of devotion to Naomi (Ruth 1:16-17). He probably befriended David when he lived in Ziklag, and his character and person appealed to Ittai to the point of his leaving his Philistine gods and coming into the land of Israel to serve the true God. Ittai's devotion to David reminds us of Paul's devotion to Christ: "For to me to live is Christ, and to die is gain" (Phil 1:21). Are we prepared to leave lands, family, or friends to serve the Lord?

Ittai was prepared to endure hardness as "a good soldier of Jesus Christ" (2 Tim 2:3). He was a warrior for the Lord and oversaw a garrison (2 Sam 18:2) which was probably composed of 600 men (1 Sam 13:15; 14:2; 23:13). He was with David in the days of his tears and sorrows. True friends are always there in our times of sorrow. Paul says that in the Assembly of God's people when "one member suffer(s), all the members suffer" (1 Cor 12:26).

Zadok – a worshipper and a watcher (2 Sam 15:24-29)

Zadok and Abaithar were both worshipping priests. They were well intentioned in seeking to stand in the Kidron with the Ark of the Covenant as David and the people passed over, just as the priests had done with the Ark in the crossing of the Jordan (2 Sam 15:23-24). But David was wise in sending the Ark back into the city (v 25). He would recall the last time the Ark was brought out of the House of God and ended up in Philistine hands. The Ark also did not need anyone to defend it – he could personally testify to this as in a place called Perezuzzah (2 Sam 6:8) he had seen Uzzah putting forth his hand to steady the Ark from falling off a cart and immediately dying, and they had all heard how in Samuel's day, in the house of Dagon, the Ark had destroyed the big fish-head god just leaving a stump without a human hand being near it (1 Sam 5:4).

The need for priestly men to stay in God's house to pray and watch and sacrifice in a day of crisis was obvious to David (vv 27-29). And so Zadok and Abiathar were sent back into the city to pray, worship and watch, and send word, via their sons Ahimaaz and Jonathan, when there was any information that could prove helpful to David. We may not feel we can do much in a crisis, but we can all pray, we can all worship, we can all watch. We can be an observer of the times and pray more effectively. We can all send messages of encouragement as we see answers to prayer. We can pray and watch out for danger and let others know. The Lord Jesus said, "Watch and pray, that ye enter not into temptation" (Matt 26:41). Paul adds, "Continue in prayer, and watch in the same with thanksgiving" (Col 4:2). Peter reminds us to "be sober (awake and in your right mind), be vigilant (alert)" (1 Peter 5:8).

May God give us help to stay completely loyal to His House even when it appears that everyone is abandoning it (1 Tim 3:15). It helps those who want to get back to right things to do so when they see the loyalty of others. The act of staying close to the Ark by Zadok and Abiathar when David is fleeing reminds us of the importance of staying close to the Lord and continuing to enjoy personal communion with Him in the dark days of crisis. Jude says, "Keep yourselves in the love of God" (v 21). We need friends who will watch and pray for us so that we keep in active devotion to the Lord in our days of trial.

Hushai the Archite – a wise counsellor (2 Sam 15:30-37; 16:15-17:21)

Ittai is known for his warring for David and Zadok for his watching, but Hushai is known for his wisdom. David hears that his good friend Ahithophel has turned against him. He writes of this dreadful treachery in Psalm 41: "Yea, mine own familiar friend, in whom I trusted, which did eat of my bread, hath lifted up his heel against me" (Ps 41:9). David prayed, "O Lord, I pray thee turn the counsel of Ahithophel into foolishness" (2 Sam 15:31). As David prays this prayer, at the top of the mountain where he worshipped, his friend Hushai suddenly appears (15:32). David feels that his prayers have been answered. Hushai is an old man and of no real use to David on the battlefield, but he could be of service to him in the board room. He sends him back to Absalom in his secret role as a fifth columnist. We cannot condone such practice today as we are never asked to do the work of the Lord by stealth. However, the principle of a hidden person, doing a work of private counsel without anyone else knowing, is a good one. Hidden counsel is a very important work: the assemblies of God's people need those who work away privately and give wise advice and support to those in the public place. "Let him that is taught in the word communicate unto him that teacheth in all good things" (Gal 6:6). Priscilla and Aquila did that hidden work of counsel with Apollos, expounding "unto him the way of God more perfectly" (Acts 18:26-28). This hidden ministry was never more needed than it is today.

Hushai's advice to Absalom about how to defeat David was accepted rather than that of Ahithophel (2 Sam 17). But God was behind this guidance: "And Absalom and all the men of Israel said, The counsel of Hushai the Archite is better than the counsel of Ahithophel. For the LORD had appointed to defeat the good counsel of Ahithophel, to the intent that the LORD might bring evil upon Absalom" (17:14). We need friends that can speak God's word in the private place. This all results in Ahithophel taking his life due to the shame of his counsel not being followed (17:23). Ahithophel was the grandfather of Bathsheba (2 Sam 11:3; 23:34) and this might be the reason he turned against David. Throwing in his lot, however, with a wicked man like Absalom and then tragically ending his own life is very sad.

A woman by a well

Hushai advises Zadok and Abiathar of his counsel to Absalom and asks that they get this message to David. David was not to stay in an open area but to flee across the Jordan as Absalom was bringing the full army of Israel against him. Being forewarned is forearmed. The priests send their sons to deliver the message to David, but a young boy informs Absalom, and they are followed and chased by Absalom's forces into a man's house in Bahurim (17:15-18). It was there a woman, who is nameless, courageously, and by sheer ingenuity, hid two of God's messengers from the servants of Absalom. She hid the men in a well (which must have been dry!) and spreading clothes over the well and putting some grain to dry on it, made it difficult for it to be examined. And, of course, when the soldiers came to find Jonathan and Ahimaaz they could not locate them allowing the two messengers of God to ultimately get to David and warn him (17:18-22).

We need friends that can aid communication and ensure that messages are sent to those in need. In a time of crisis companions like these are invaluable. We little know what a phone call, text, short visit, letter can do to help people who are suffering.

Women by wells are always good at refreshing the hearts of God's people. Rebekah gave water to the servant of Abraham and to his camels and was unaware that she was answering the prayer of the servant (Gen 24). The woman at the well in John 4 spread the good news of the "Christ" into Samaria having received "living water". This unnamed woman by the well is also representative of the hidden work of our sisters, encouraging and supporting the work of God. Peter writes of friends like her: "But let it be the hidden man of the heart, in that which is not corruptible, even the ornament of a meek and quiet spirit, which is in the sight of God of great price" (1 Peter 3:4). Dorcas is another example of people like her making clothes for the poor (Acts 9). Jehoshabeath hiding Joash from Athaliah (2 Chron 22), and the daughters of Shallum repairing the walls with little recognition are another two good examples (Neh 3:12). When Paul boarded a boat at Caesarea (Acts 9:30) he needed to be hidden, fed, watered, and transported. We need friends who can aid us, support us, and keep the lines of communication open when we are in a time of crisis. This work is indispensable.

Barzillai - a warmer of hearts

David has now made his base in Mahanaim. His men are faint and need food, shelter and sleep. The battle is looming, and Absalom is already in Gilead with "all the men of Israel". What did they need? They needed encouragement and practical support. We all need encouragers - people who support the saints financially and practically. Barzillai was such a man. He (and others) "Brought beds, and basins, and earthen vessels, and wheat, and barley, and flour, and parched corn, and beans, and lentiles, and parched pulse, And honey, and butter, and sheep, and cheese of kine, for David, and for the people that were with him, to eat: for they said, The people is hungry, and weary, and thirsty, in the wilderness" (17:28-29). He was like the Philippian believers of whom Paul said, "For even in Thessalonica ye sent once and again unto my necessity" (Phil 4:16), and Phebe who was a "succourer of many" (Rom 16:2). We need companions like these. It is through people like Barzillai, who use their resources to bless others, that the work of God is maintained. Paul encourages those who have wealth: "That they do good, that they be rich in good works, ready to distribute, willing to communicate; Laying up in store for themselves a good foundation against the time to come, that they may lay hold on eternal life" (1 Tim 6:17-19). The Macedonian assemblies were "Barzillai-like" for the poor in Jerusalem (2 Cor 8 and 9). We should all endeavour to be warmers of the saints' hearts like this whenever they are in need.

An unnamed man – unwavering obedience

The sign of true friendship is when we obey requests even when friends are not able to see us or know what we are doing. David had an unnamed servant who did just that. David had warned everyone not to kill Absalom. This man saw Absalom riding upon a mule and his head getting caught in an oak tree and Absalom hanging there. Every sinew of his body must have strained to kill Absalom, but he did not and simply told Joab what he had seen. Humble obedience is always best even if we think there is a better way. He followed the King's orders. We all might think that we could do this or that in a crisis – the trouble is that our ideas might be unscriptural. We might think we know what the right thing is to do, but it is always best to follow the King's orders. Moses warns, "Only take heed to thyself, and keep thy soul diligently, lest thou forget the things which thine eyes have seen, and lest they depart from thy heart all the days of thy life: but teach them thy sons, and thy sons' sons" (Deut 4:9). The Lord Jesus said, "If ye love me, keep my commandments ... If ye keep my commandments, ye shall abide in my love; even as I have kept my Father's commandments, and abide in his love" (John 14:10; 15:9-10). It is always best to obey.

Joab said that the man could have been rewarded had he killed Absalom, but this unnamed friend would take no gift as he had heard the King say, "Beware that none touch the young man Absalom" (18:9-13). There might be those who tell us to disobey our leaders, and might even promise influence and reward, but Scripture says: "Obey them that have the rule over you, and submit yourselves: for they watch for your souls, as they that must give account, that they may do it with joy, and not with grief: for that is unprofitable for you" (Heb 13:17). Obedience will always be blessed.

Joab's actions in killing Absalom whilst the latter was hanging in the tree had major ramifications and resulted his being removed as Captain which, in turn, caused him to murder his rival Amasa in act of jealousy (2 Sam 20:8-10). The way of the transgressor is hard.

Ahimaaz – a willing witness (2 Sam 18:19-29)

Ahimaaz was a man who was willing to run to David and bear witness to what had happened in the forest. God had overruled the usurpation of Absalom, and Ahimaaz wanted to bear witness to David of God's goodness.

People who bear witness need to have a character consistent with their message. People may forget what you said, but they never forget how you made them feel as you said it. David said of Ahimaaz, "He is a good man, and cometh with good tidings" (18:27). People who are willing to work for the Lord must also be wise and pleasant with it and have the moral authority to speak.

Ahimaaz was recognised by his running (18:27)! It is good when people know us for our enthusiasm. He was determined to outrun Cushi as he did not want the King to hear the news in a bad way (18:25). Joab told Cushi to tell David "what he had seen" – this was callous and cruel as Cushi had seen the slaying of Absalom. We have to be truthful, but we need to be wise. And we also need to be able to hold our counsel. Ahimaaz had told the King bad news before (17:19-21) and knew the importance of motive and method in delivering a message, but that day there was also some very good news, and he was determined to bear this news first to the King. Are we willing to run so that God's word can be spread in the right way? Are we willing to go the second mile? Paul said, "And whatsoever ye do, do it heartily, as to the Lord, and not unto men" (Col 3:23). We need enthusiasm, but we also need courage as sometimes we must speak of things that can be unpalatable but are necessary. The Lord said, "... ye shall be witnesses unto me" (Acts 1:8). Let us rise to this challenge.

Conclusion

This incredible episode in David's life reminds us of the types of companions that helped him in crises, and still help us today when we pass through deep waters. There were those who fought for him like Ittai, others that prayed for him like Zadok, people that spoke up for him like Hushai, or helped him by ensuring he was kept up to date like the woman at the well. Then there were others that fed and supported him materially like Barzillai, or an unnamed man that simply obeyed him and stayed loyal even if he was not there to see it, and finally people that ran for him, like Ahimaaz, simply to be a witness to good news in order to encourage him. As the Scriptures teach: "A friend loveth at all times" (Prov 17:17).

PSALM 3

[A Psalm of David, when he fled from Absalom his son.]

¹ LORD, how are they increased that trouble me! many are they that rise up against me.

² Many there be which say of my soul, There is no help for him in God. Selah.

³ But thou, O LORD, art a shield for me; my glory, and the lifter up of mine head.

⁴ I cried unto the LORD with my voice, and he heard me out of his holy hill. Selah.

⁵ I laid me down and slept; I awaked; for the LORD sustained me.

⁶ I will not be afraid of ten thousands of people, that have set themselves against me round about.

⁷ Arise, O LORD; save me, O my God: for thou hast smitten all mine enemies upon the cheek bone; thou hast broken the teeth of the ungodly.

⁸ Salvation belongeth unto the LORD: thy blessing is upon thy people. Selah.

CHAPTER 16

David: His Comeback

2 Samuel 19

Absalom is dead. The attack is over. Getting back to "normal" for David should be easy! But is it? He does ultimately return to Jerusalem and the Kingdom is restored in this chapter, but the journey back is of interest to us. We hope to learn lessons of restoration from the friends that helped David back to the palace, and the barriers that require to be overcome for corporate unity to be restored.

Some people have lost confidence in David and have accepted some of the propaganda of Absalom which is seen in the debate that is ongoing on David's fitness to lead, "And all the people were at strife throughout all the tribes of Israel" (2 Sam 19:9). Others fully support David, even those who had previously favoured Absalom, saying, "... why speak ye not a word of bringing the king back?" (2 Sam 19:10). Some of David's own men had not behaved themselves as they should have done, including Joab, one of his three commanders. People were wary, watching to see who had the greatest influence over David, especially if they had formerly been loyal to Absalom. David's conduct at this time was critical.

There are lessons here about how we get back again as God's people after division. The first lesson is to not get involved in the type of tittle tattle highlighted in vv 9-10. We can bite and devour one another very easily in the aftermath of a crisis. We are reminded of Paul's warning to the Galatian assemblies where Judaising teachers were causing strife: "But if ye bite and devour one another, take heed that ye be not consumed one of another" (Gal 5:15). We will look at David's journey back to Jerusalem, therefore, from a practical point of view and observe principles about restoration that will centre around the individuals that David meets on his return.

Fire flamed

David wanted the whole of Israel to get back together. He was determined to see unity and the Kingdom restored. Restoration required determined action, but for David to realise this vision he required the help of priestly men. And so, we read: "And king David sent to Zadok and to Abiathar the priests, saying, Speak unto the elders of Judah, saying, Why are ye the last to bring the king back to his house? seeing the speech of all Israel (talk of the town!) is come to the king, even to his house. Ye are my brethren, ye are my bones and my flesh: wherefore then are ye the last to bring back the king?" (2 Sam 19:11-12).

The house of Judah should have been the first to want David to be back. They were his own kith and kin as he said, "... my bones and my flesh". Sometimes barriers can come from the most unusual areas. People who have been on the road a long time together and love the Assembly and can prevaricate at the very time they need to act decisively. Sometimes it is fear or psychological issues, and priestly people are needed to help fellow saints make the right decisions.

David didn't send for the Pelethites to help the elders of Judah; he sent for the priests. Peter wrote of elders: "Neither as being lords over God's heritage, but being ensamples to the flock" (1 Peter 5:3). It takes godly men who have the confidence of others to restore saints to the fold of the assembly. Elders should not be quick to judge or appropriate blame but need to tenderly work through issues to bring those who have left the fold back into its safety. We must pray that the fire will return, and the spark of hope be kindled, and we hear our brethren and sisters once again say, "I was glad when they said unto me, let us go into the house of the LORD" (Ps 122:1).

Fears quelled

David is not unaware of what people were thinking and is not afraid of addressing the issues directly. He is teaching us the importance of dealing with the real fears of our brothers and sisters and not trying to ignore them. Joab had behaved badly in killing Absalom against

David's orders. He was so ruthless that even David's armies would have been afraid of him. Those who had been loyal to Absalom must have worried about reprisals by Joab and may have wondered if they would have any place in David's thoughts. David's choice of the man to be the leader of the unified army was going to be critical. He had to appoint an impartial captain who could be trusted by both sides for the country to be united.

The decisions leaders take reveal their priorities. Who, then, is to be captain of the Army? Joab - an incredible warrior, but he was not chosen by David due to his behaviour with Absalom and his character. Abishai - he is a very brave man but might be seen as being too close to his brother Joab as is shown to be the case in chapter 20. Ittai - a wonderful warrior who was loyal to David, but would Israel ever accept a Philistine in charge? Also, we do not read of him again – perhaps he had been killed in battle. David makes a very bold decision, some would say a premature and unwise decision, to appoint Amasa (Absalom's commander) as his captain.

"And say ye to Amasa, Art thou not of my bone, and of my flesh? God do so to me, and more also, if thou be not captain of the host before me continually in the room of Joab. And he bowed the heart of all the men of Judah, even as the heart of one man; so that they sent this word unto the king, Return thou, and all thy servants. So the king returned, and came to Jordan. And Judah came to Gilgal, to go to meet the king, to conduct the king over Jordan" (2 Sam 19:13-15).

Whatever view we take of Amasa as captain, the basic principle of "peace making" by David is a good one. Actively engaging brothers and sisters who may feel ostracised by recent events and worry about their acceptance is a righteous and wise move. The results here are dramatic – "... he bowed the heart of all the men of Judah, even as the heart of one man" (v 14). David later wrote: "Behold, how good and how pleasant it is for brethren to dwell together in unity!" (Ps 133:1). People want to know that they will be accepted if they come on board, and conciliatory decisions such as this help to unite God's people.

Forgiveness given

Gilgal was chosen as the crossing point over Jordan for David and his army to come back to Jerusalem. Perhaps this was because of the availability of the ferry. It is just at this point, when David is crossing, that Shimei turns up! And he just doesn't turn up alone or quietly but fords the river before him with a thousand Benjamites to greet David. He runs towards David and falls at his feet whenever he landed on the eastern shore (19:16-18)! David's heart must have sunk. It would have been difficult for him to look at Shimei in the face never mind facing him in this highly public place. He had been wicked to David in 2 Samuel 16:5-13. His slander dug far more deeply than the stones he threw at David.

People who slander do not know the searing pain that they cause. There must have been every temptation by David to punish him, and many believe that David was weak here and should have executed him immediately. If, however, David had slain him at this time, there would have been a message sent out that the "retaliation" war had started. Others would be running to the hills to escape. The message they would have believed was that forgiveness was impossible with David. That does not make it any easier on David at this point - in fact the pressure builds up on him. The cost of forgiveness is a big subject. It cost our Lord Jesus everything to forgive us.

What do you do when a man, like Shimei, begs forgiveness from you? Shimei said to David: "Let not my lord impute iniquity unto me, neither do thou remember that which thy servant did perversely the day that my lord the king went out of Jerusalem, that the king should take it to his heart. For thy servant doth know that I have sinned: therefore, behold, I am come the first this day of all the house of Joseph to go down to meet my lord the king" (19:19-20). The answer, however painful, is to pray for grace to forgive. We can only forgive in the measure that we have been forgiven: "Let all bitterness, and wrath, and anger, and clamour, and evil speaking, be put away from you, with all malice: And be ye kind one to another, tenderhearted, forgiving one another, even as God for Christ's sake hath forgiven you" (Eph 4:31-32). And how are we forgiven by the Lord? – unconditionally, personally, and eternally.

Abishai knew nothing of this forgiveness. He wanted Shimei's head taken off at the time of his rebellious behaviour, and his wishes had not changed (16:9; 19:21-22). But David was teaching him that forgiveness is an act of the will, and in promising Shimei that he was forgiven (19:23) he sent a message out to the whole of Israel that he, David, was not motivated by retaliation. This helped heal the nation. Forgiveness still heals divisions.

Now, perhaps David, whilst promising Shimei he would not die, should have placed him on some form of probation, as Solomon did later in 1 Kings 2:36-38. Forgiveness is immediate and final, but trust in positions of responsibility takes time to be regained. It is not always the case, for example, that people can resume the same responsibilities in an assembly immediately after they have been restored. This may be a case in which David could have gone further; however, the principle of forgiveness is still a huge one which David has learned.

Forgiving others is the demonstration that we have been forgiven ourselves (Matt 18:21-35). If we fail to forgive others, then we are out of communion with God and we will not be able to enjoy His forgiveness. If we continue to not forgive others and live our life in this way, then it is a sure sign we have never been born again and forgiven at all. Repentance is the condition of being forgiven, and the temper that does not forgive is incompatible with the temper of the penitent. In other words, an unforgiving spirit is the mark of an unsaved individual (Matt 6:15). Some people are harder to forgive than others, but we must still forgive. May we, like David, be given help to forgive. There is no other way.

Feuds settled

The next person that meets David as he crosses Jordan is Mephibosheth who had made his way the 18 miles to Gilgal, despite his disability. He had not cut his nails, his hair, or trimmed his beard since David left. So loyal was he to David that he was in perpetual mourning since David left the palace. David was too quick to accept Ziba's story of why Mephibosheth had not come (16:1-4), perhaps influenced by Ziba's gifts at a time of crisis. He was also too quick to give the inheritance to Ziba. This is lesson for us today - we can all be taken in by people with ulterior motives. Paul writes, "Some men's sins are open beforehand", i.e., they are obvious, and others that "they follow after", i.e., they become apparent after time and investigation (1 Tim 5:24). Be cautious before accepting stories of people's sin.

David was also too quick to go for a compromise about the "inheritance" when he met Mephibosheth, saying, "Thou and Ziba divide the land" between you (19:29). Mephibosheth's reaction is incredible: "Yea, let him take all, forasmuch as my lord the king is come again in peace unto his own house" (19:30). This outstanding response by Mephibosheth reminds us of the words of the Apostle Paul: "Yea doubtless, and I count all things but loss for the excellency of the knowledge of Christ Jesus my Lord: for whom I have suffered the loss of all things, and do count them but dung, that I may win Christ" (Phil 3:8). Mephibosheth's love for the King means he will accept any loss, although he had many witnesses to prove his case that he had always been loyal to David. He never forgot what David did for him: "For all of my father's house were but dead men before my lord the king: yet didst thou set thy servant among them that did eat at thine own table. What right therefore have I yet to cry any more unto the king?" (19:28). His foregoing of his rights and his willingness to be defrauded reminds us of the problem in Corinth when they were taking each other to court: "Why do ye not rather take wrong? why do ye not rather suffer yourselves to be defrauded?" (1 Cor 6:7).

When you have a person like Mephibosheth feuds soon disappear. His love for the King helped him overcome even when he was personally wronged. We have discovered that we can behave very badly if a problem affects our finances. It should not. It is sin. We should be ready to sacrifice for the Lord and His House. Mephibosheth was able to shave and change his clothes because the King was back in *his* house. How much does the House of God mean to us, and the honour of the Name of His Son? Would we accept loss for His sake and for the place of the Name?

We learn then from this episode with Mephibosheth the importance of listening to both sides and properly analysing the data before we come to conclusions. We also learn that sometimes the people that are labelled "unspiritual" are incredibly "spiritual". It takes time to know. In this case, Mephibosheth's unkempt face was a sign of deep affection for David, not disloyalty!

Finally, we learn that when people are willing to be defrauded and take the low place then feuds are easily resolved, and peace is enjoyed.

Future secured

The last person to conduct David over the Jordan was Barzillai the Gileadite (19:31). Over the period of the crisis, it had become apparent to Barzillai that his days were drawing to an end, and he could not do what he used to be able to do. He had, at great personal risk to himself, supported David in exile and now he is "a very aged man" (19:32). He reminds us of the first century, AD, when Christians who were exposed to huge dangers and financial penalties took "joyfully the spoiling of [their] goods" (Heb 10:34).

David never forgot Barzillai's kindness or the personal risk he took for him and asks him to join him in the escort over the river and on the first leg of his journey. He then invites him to come and stay with him permanently (19:33). Barzillai, however, feels he is too old to go with David and be his houseguest. He recognises that his discernment is not what it used to be, and he does not feel that he would be of value to David as a counsellor. He could not enjoy David's food as his taste buds had gone. He could not even enjoy the singing and the fellowship, for his hearing had also failed (19:34-37). Instead, he said he had been preparing Chimham for this task. It is good when an older man has an eye to the future (19:38-40) and encourages a rising generation that need to take up opportunity and responsibility. Barzillai wants to give Chimham the prospect of serving in the Palace – he would not be a "Barzillai" overnight, but he might grow up to rise higher than any of his fathers.

Paul had the same desire for Timothy: "And the things that thou hast heard of me among many witnesses, the same commit thou to faithful men, who shall be able to teach others also" (2 Tim 2:2); "Let no man despise thy youth; but be thou an example of the believers, in word, in conversation, in charity, in spirit, in faith, in purity" (1 Tim 4:12). For this to work, the Barzillais of this world have to be accessible and the Chimhams need to be available. Thankfully, Paul was accessible, and Timothy was available and gave himself wholly to it, studying to show himself "approved unto God" (2 Tim 2:15). If we are to have unity fully established amongst God's people, we must see that there are no generation gaps, and that young people learn from the older, more experienced, saints. Space must also be given for the younger people to develop and to take responsibility.

Conclusion

In conclusion, if we are to see unity established amongst God's people, we will need to fan the flames of enthusiasm for restoration, and deal with the real fears of believers. This will require priestly sensitivity and impartiality. We must show forgiveness and go out of our way to resolve feuds, if necessary being willing to be "defrauded" like Mephibosheth for the greater good. Leaders of God's people must also keep old and young together and not allow division on the grounds of age. Finally, leaders must be willing to pass on the legacy of truth to a rising generation.

PSALM 7

*[Shiggaion of David, which he sang unto the LORD,
concerning the words of Cush the Benjamite.]*

(Cush the Benjamite is most likely Shimei.)

¹ O LORD my God, in thee do I put my trust: save me from all them that persecute me, and deliver me:

² Lest he tear my soul like a lion, rending it in pieces, while there is none to deliver.

³ O LORD my God, if I have done this; if there be iniquity in my hands;

⁴ If I have rewarded evil unto him that was at peace with me; (yea, I have delivered him that without cause is mine enemy:)

⁵ Let the enemy persecute my soul, and take it; yea, let him tread down my life upon the earth, and lay mine honour in the dust. Selah.

⁶ Arise, O LORD, in thine anger, lift up thyself because of the rage of mine enemies: and awake for me to the judgment that thou hast commanded.

⁷ So shall the congregation of the people compass thee about: for their sakes therefore return thou on high.

⁸ The LORD shall judge the people: judge me, O LORD, according to my righteousness, and according to mine integrity that is in me.

⁹ Oh let the wickedness of the wicked come to an end; but

establish the just: for the righteous God trieth the hearts and reins.

¹⁰ My defence is of God, which saveth the upright in heart.

¹¹ God judgeth the righteous, and God is angry with the wicked every day.

¹² If he turn not, he will whet his sword; he hath bent his bow, and made it ready.

¹³ He hath also prepared for him the instruments of death; he ordaineth his arrows against the persecutors.

¹⁴ Behold, he travaileth with iniquity, and hath conceived mischief, and brought forth falsehood.

¹⁵ He made a pit, and digged it, and is fallen into the ditch which he made.

¹⁶ His mischief shall return upon his own head, and his violent dealing shall come down upon his own pate.

¹⁷ I will praise the LORD according to his righteousness: and will sing praise to the name of the LORD most high.

CHAPTER 17

David: The Consequences of the Past

2 Samuel 20-21

Unfinished business

In chapters 20 and 21 we read of unfinished business. Matters that should have been resolved years before now rear their heads again. In chapter 20 the old north/south division in the Kingdom, exacerbated by Sheba, needed to be healed and the relationship with Joab and David resolved. In chapter 21, the bones of Saul require to be buried, the sons of Goliath must be slain, and the legacy of sin against the Gibeonites by Saul needs to be judged. We learn in this section that our behaviour in the past has implications for the present.

In Joab's case, his behaviour was not addressed, and this had to be resolved after David's reign. However, the usurpation of Sheba is quelled, the bones of past disputes are buried, and the Philistine aggression is removed, and will remain so for some considerable time.

These chapters, therefore, outline the unfinished business that David passed to Solomon and the unfinished business that David inherited, both impacting upon unity and justice. It is encouraging to remember that our blessed Lord Jesus uniquely "finished the work" before He left this world (John 17:4). He left nothing undone. May we seek to learn lessons from these chapters so that we do not make the same mistakes and pass on to another generation unfinished business.

Old divisions (2 Sam 20:1-3)

If we do not deal with old divisions, they tend to come back in some form or another. In chapter 20, Sheba, criticising David and encouraging Israel to rebel against the Judean King, was really a new man revealing an old, unresolved issue. Sheba is exposing the north/ south divide in the country and saying that the northern tribes "have no part in David". He had seen the divisions at first hand in the previous chapter where the men of Israel vied for the closest connection with David as King: "And the men of Israel answered the men of Judah, and said, We have ten parts in the king, and we have also more right in David than ye: why then did ye despise us, that our advice should not be first had in bringing back our king? And the words of the men of Judah were fiercer than the words of the men of Israel" (2 Sam 19:43).

It is amazing how petty we can be at times! Not answering a text, not taking a call, not shaking the hand, standing afar off from our brothers and sisters are all examples of petty and divisive behaviours. They are unbecoming of any believer. The men of Israel are saying to the men of Judah, "Who is closest to the King?". A similar conversation took place amongst the disciples centuries later when they discussed the question, "Who should be the greatest?" (Mark 9:34).

Sheba was simply an opportunist who exploited this situation to his own advantage. He was not the cause of this division; he just exploited it and made it worse: "And there happened to be there a man of Belial, whose name was Sheba, the son of Bichri, a Benjamite: and he blew a trumpet, and said, We have no part in David, neither have we inheritance in the son of Jesse: every man to his tents, O Israel" (2 Sam 20:1). The Shebas of this world love to exploit tensions and issues. Very often those who sow division target our weakest point. In other words, there is truth in what they say, which is why it makes it more difficult to handle. However, we must not allow people to exacerbate known problems.

Notice the tactics that Sheba employs. First, he picks an issue which he knows people feel strongly about and plays on it. In this case it was a territorial question. We need to be aware that people can play on our prejudices and cause us to think ill of even our friends as a result. We see this approach in the Galatian church who were using the tendency of Jewish Christians to think favourably of the law to insist that circumcision was necessary. This was driving a wedge between the ethnicities of the Christians.

Secondly, Sheba portrays David as a "son of Jesse" and never gives him his place as the "King". He is attempting to separate Judah from Israel in order to gain a following. False leaders such as Sheba often try to wean the saints from their true mentors by privately speaking disparagingly of them. Look out for those who speak ill of those who care for God's people.

Whenever there has been a crisis in leadership, as there was with Absalom's usurpation, old divisions often emerge. As believers, let us seek to be peace makers - "Blessed are the peacemakers", exhorted the Lord Jesus (Matt 5:9). We need to be on our guard not to unwittingly make people feel as if they don't fit. We need to be inclusive and never allow a club mentality to develop amongst us. It is vital that everyone feels welcome to our homes and in the Assembly, but also that we must be on the lookout for false teachers creeping in unawares. Sheba did not blow a trumpet immediately. He had been working behind the scenes for some time in private before he publicly denounced David.

This division predates Sheba by many thousands of years. This old partition extends as far back as when Ephraim and Judah were alive, and the blessing they received from their father Jacob (Genesis 49). Both these tribes were very large and dominated the north and south of Israel, so much so that the south was called Judea and the grouping of the northern ten tribes was often called Ephraim. Divisions erupted in Gideon's day (Judges 8:1-2), in Jepthah's day (Judges 12:4) and in David's day. It came to a head in 1 Kings 12 when ten tribes went one way and the remaining two remained loyal to the Lord. Eventually, God used the Assyrians to remove the northern tribes. This division will not be completely healed until the Lord comes. Isaiah prophesies: "And he shall set up an ensign for the nations, and shall assemble the outcasts of Israel, and gather together the dispersed of Judah from the four corners of the earth. The envy also of Ephraim shall depart, and the adversaries of Judah shall be cut off: Ephraim shall not envy Judah, and Judah shall not vex Ephraim" (Isa 11:12-13). Ezekiel affirms this healing of the tribes when the Messiah returns (Ezek 37:16-19). It is sad that it could not have been resolved before this day.

Old relationships (2 Sam 20:4-23)

David wisely seeks to deal promptly with this rebellion by Sheba and uses Amasa to gather the people together. Unfortunately, Amasa seems to take an inordinate amount of time to muster the army. The former captain of Absalom is perhaps showing his inexperience. Amasa was still learning and had been thrust into this responsibility prematurely due to Joab's sin. People in this situation need encouragement in their role. This has happened in many Assemblies either through death, people moving away, or assembly discipline, and as a result, individuals have been thrust into leadership roles at a young age. We need to help believers and not hinder them in such situations. There are some brethren who will never lift their head again because of the way they were treated in their younger years.

Abishai is called in by David to help muster the people and he ought to have supported Amasa. Instead, as has been the case before, his brother Joab joins him unbidden and assumes responsibility. Amasa is sadly murdered by a cunning Joab, who could brook no rival. Amasa is killed in an uncannily similar way to the slaying of Abner (2 Sam 3). David, tragically, seems powerless to deal with Joab's cold-blooded murder. This was altogether wrong.

It is so sad when sluggishness by one brother (Amasa) and a lack of support by another brother (Abishai) allows an alternative, more carnal person, like Joab to gain a foothold. It is even more sad when previous failures allow a carnal man to act in a completely dishonourable way and be seemingly untouchable. Sometimes in dealing with one problem a secondary issue can emerge which is bigger than the original concern. David knew that Joab had a letter written by his hand that spelt the death warrant for Uriah the Hittite. David was therefore compromised in dealing with him. It would be his son Solomon that would have to handle Joab (1 Kings 2:28-35). This was one of David's many "unfinished businesses" that he handed on to the next generation. Sadly, this story has often been repeated, but it need not be the case.

Abishai and Joab besiege the city of Abel where Sheba was hiding, building earth mounts to pound the city and scale the walls. They look intent on creating another war. Our sisters can often see the problem the brethren fail to sort to support unity. The solution to the problem of Sheba was a wise woman - this can often be the case. The books of Samuel record a number of examples of such – Hannah at a time of weakness in the temple (1 Sam 1-2); Abigail in a day of David's anger (1 Sam 25); a woman by a well in the day of Absalom's rebellion (2 Sam 17); and now a wise woman in the town of Abel who, hearing why Abishai and his men were chasing Sheba, has the wisdom to see what needs to be done. She is a mother in Israel and had an appreciation of the inheritance of the Lord. She speaks spiritual words to Joab: "I am one of them that are peaceable and faithful in Israel: thou seekest to destroy a city and a mother in Israel: why wilt thou swallow up the inheritance of the LORD?" (2 Sam 20:19). She had a clear understanding that the land belonged to the Lord (Lev 25:23). She also has the personal authority and wisdom for her advice to be heard by the elders in Abel. Sheba was subsequently judged for his treason and lost his life. This prevented a blood bath and saved many other lives. The outcome of peace is achieved, and the usurpation is over. Sisters, whilst not in a position of leadership (and no one should seek to lead the Assembly by proxy through their husbands) can, through godly advice and life, help the people of God. This is especially powerful if the advice is given in the spirit of humility and love.

Old sins (2 Sam 21:1-10)

The problem in chapter 21 related to an issue that David had inherited, namely the injustice of Saul to the Gibeonites. The Gibeonites (who were Hivites) had been given a solemn covenant promise by Joshua (Joshua 9:16-27) that they would become servants to Israel and never treated as enemies. The incredible story of their deception driven through fear, and then their deliverance and promised protection is found in the remaining parts of Joshua 9. Saul, however, ignored this covenant promise and slew them. Saul who had trouble slaying the real enemies, the Amalekites, had no problem putting to the sword people who, by covenant, were promised friendship with Israel. This great injustice needed to be resolved and of course it demanded punishment for those who had offended. David clearly regarded this sin as an iniquity which had polluted the land: "So ye shall not pollute the land wherein ye are: for blood it defileth the land: and the land cannot be cleansed of the blood that is shed therein, but by the blood of him that shed it" (Num 35:33). David, although not personally responsible, possibly felt the need to take action that they might be able to "bless the inheritance of the Lord" (2 Sam 21:3). Would that all of us had the same approach.

The Gibeonites response about what they wished to happen, and their subsequent actions, is hard to read, and is certainly unscriptural. They asked for seven men of Saul's seed to be killed and hung for public humiliation. It is disgusting to read of bodies being left to the elements and the birds, and this was completely contrary to God's Word: "His body shall not remain all night upon the tree, but thou shalt in any wise bury him that day; (for he that is hanged is accursed of God;) that thy land be not defiled, which the LORD thy God giveth thee for an inheritance" (Deut 21:22-23). These men were refused a proper burial, displaying a public example of retribution for the crime against the Gibeonites.

The seven men who were hung up to die were of the seed of Saul and they may have been involved in the slaughter of the Gibeonites. David had promised to look after Jonathan's seed so Mephibosheth was spared, but another Mephibosheth was slain. The Gibeonites were wrong to demand such a resolution, but the principle that we will reap what we sow is certainly found here. Saul and his progeny lived by the sword and now they would die by the sword. The other principle of being seen to put matters right was clearly important to David

Why this tragic incident is allowed by the Lord to happen is not explained. Like so much of life there are many things we do not understand now, but we will one day (John 13:7). One possibility is that with Saul's dynasty over, the seed of Saul might have been the residue of resentment in David's Kingdom and were perhaps secretly plotting to take the Kingdom back. The fact that five of the seven slain were of Michal's seed in her unlawful marriage to Adriel the Meholathite might suggest that these sons were not neutral in the division of Saul and David and were anti-David by practice and position. It could be that God overrules this by permitting the Gibeonite's unjust actions and yet using this to bring about righteous judgment upon Saul's seed, so preserving the Kingdom. If this was the case it would be similar to the judgment of God on the people as a result of David's sin in numbering the people (2 Sam 24). There was obviously a greater sin or sins that God was dealing with at that time. God can and does make the wrath of man to praise Him (Ps 76:10).

Although Scripture does not tell us why this happened, what is certainly the case is that Saul's seed is removed and in the next section the Philistine's progeny is destroyed, both having plagued Israel since the start of the Kingdom. This perhaps illustrates the truth of Ephesians 1:11 of God "who worketh all things after the counsel of his own will". Sometimes the Lord resolves the problems of the past for us, and sometimes He does this through the haphazard and fickle ways of men who are unaware that God can use even their mistakes to carry out His ultimate purpose.

Old bones (2 Sam 21:11-14)

David was moved and inspired by Rizpah, the mother of two of the men killed, mourning and standing vigil over the bodies and honouring the dead. Rizpah guards the bodies for six months – from April (barley harvest) to October (when rains came). David now wants to deal honourably, once and for all, with the bodies of Saul and Jonathan. He endeavours to bury the bones of Saul which should have been done years before. He brings them from Jabesh-gilead and buries them in the land of Benjamin, in the grave of Kish, Saul's father. Saul's behaviour towards David had been appalling, but this crisis provides opportunity to completely bury the bones of the past and move on -

it is liberating! There is no such thing as, "I will forgive but I cannot forget!" We must bury the bones of previous disputes which can often remain divisive long after men are dead.

Old enemies (2 Sam 21:15-22)

There was one issue that David started that he did finish – the Philistines. David took five stones out of the brook for a reason in 1 Samuel 17, but he only used one on Goliath. It seems reasonable to believe that the four sons of Goliath were there, but they were undefeated (since only one stone was used) and the Philistines would keep troubling Israel. The four sons of Goliath are all killed here (v 22), and David almost kills himself in the process (v 16). Abishai saved David, and his brethren preserved him calling him "the light of Israel" (v 17). We are not home to glory yet - the victories of our youth can become the scenes of failure in old age. It is wonderful when our brethren seek to protect us when we are vulnerable and faint.

We do not read of the Philistines being a problem to Solomon as they had been for generations previously. In fact, the Philistines brought Solomon presents: "And Solomon reigned over all kingdoms from the river unto the land of the Philistines, and unto the border of Egypt: they brought presents, and served Solomon all the days of his life" (1 Kings 4:21). We never read of them arising again until hundreds of years later in the reign of Uzziah in 2 Chronicles 26.

Conclusion

Closure is a wonderful thing and resolution is now accomplished in relation to Sheba, the Gibeonites, and the Philistines. These chapters, therefore, remind us of the importance of burying the bones of the past, eliminating giants that have been spared, and dealing with the sins of a previous generation. It is amazing how, in times of crisis, issues from the past come back to haunt us! We must, therefore, seek to put matters right that need to be dealt with, heal division, and resolve in our hearts that we will not pass on our unfished business to another generation.

PSALM 139

[To the chief Musician, A Psalm of David.]

¹ O LORD, thou hast searched me, and known me.

² Thou knowest my downsitting and mine uprising, thou understandest my thought afar off.

³ Thou compassest my path and my lying down, and art acquainted with all my ways.

⁴ For there is not a word in my tongue, but, lo, O LORD, thou knowest it altogether.

⁵ Thou hast beset me behind and before, and laid thine hand upon me.

⁶ Such knowledge is too wonderful for me; it is high, I cannot attain unto it.

⁷ Whither shall I go from thy spirit? or whither shall I flee from thy presence?

⁸ If I ascend up into heaven, thou art there: if I make my bed in hell, behold, thou art there.

⁹ If I take the wings of the morning, and dwell in the uttermost parts of the sea;

¹⁰ Even there shall thy hand lead me, and thy right hand shall hold me.

¹¹ If I say, Surely the darkness shall cover me; even the night shall be light about me.

¹² Yea, the darkness hideth not from thee; but the night shineth as the day: the darkness and the light are both alike to thee.

¹³ For thou hast possessed my reins: thou hast covered me in my mother's womb.

¹⁴ I will praise thee; for I am fearfully and wonderfully made: marvellous are thy works; and that my soul knoweth right well.

¹⁵ My substance was not hid from thee, when I was made in secret, and curiously wrought in the lowest parts of the earth.

¹⁶ Thine eyes did see my substance, yet being unperfect; and in thy book all my members were written, which in continuance were fashioned, when as yet there was none of them.

¹⁷ How precious also are thy thoughts unto me, O God! how great is the sum of them!

¹⁸ If I should count them, they are more in number than the sand: when I awake, I am still with thee.

¹⁹ Surely thou wilt slay the wicked, O God: depart from me therefore, ye bloody men.

²⁰ For they speak against thee wickedly, and thine enemies take thy name in vain.

²¹ Do not I hate them, O LORD, that hate thee? and am not I grieved with those that rise up against thee?

²² I hate them with perfect hatred: I count them mine enemies.

²³ Search me, O God, and know my heart: try me, and know my thoughts:

²⁴ And see if there be any wicked way in me, and lead me in the way everlasting.

CHAPTER 18

David: The Cost of Counting

2 Samuel 23b-24

Here we learn about true value. We have the names of the mighty men and some of the costly actions they took out of love for David. There are some surprising additions and omissions in the list of these mighty men. In chapter 24 we have the numbering of the army and the judgment that comes upon David and the people as result. The juxtaposition of the names of those who sacrificed for David along with the vexed issue of numbering is intriguing. God is interested not so much in numbers but in people that can be counted upon, that is, those who are reliable. The judgment that falls in chapter 24 reminds us of the cost of sin. The section ends with the purchase of the threshing floor of Araunah the Jebusite, for the House of God. The value of the House of God is underlined in these chapters. The very spot where Isaac was offered on the altar, Mount Moriah, is the place at which the Lord identified that His House was to be built.

In chapter 23 we have the names of David's mighty men. We learn the value of these men who fought for David - the value of service. It is a little reminder to us of the Judgment Seat of Christ and how divine appraisal and reward will work.

In chapter 24 we have numbers. We see the grave sin of David counting the size of his army. It teaches us the value of simplicity and dependency upon God and the danger of pride.

At the end of chapter 24 we see, in the threshing floor of Ornan (Araunah) the Jebusite, the value of sacrifice and the sanctuary. David pays the price for the threshingfloor, and a greater amount for the whole of the temple mount.

The mighty men (2 Samuel 23:8-39)

The value of service

David never looked for personal glory. He gave all the glory to the Lord and paid due credit to his men who had been with him. Their service is fully recognised by David just as we should recognise the service of others. These men were all inspired to work for David and we are inspired to work for our Lord Jesus. In some ways the listing of names in this chapter, as in Nehemiah 3 and Romans 16 is a little picture of the Judgment Seat of Christ. Our conflicts for Christ (2 Samuel 23), our work (Nehemiah 3), and our burden for one another (Romans 16) will all be assessed and rewarded in a coming day. So, what is going to be rewarded? David's list gives us an insight into the value of service for the King.

The Lord values courage in service

The first of David's men is called Adino the Eznite, or Jashobeam, or Josheb-Basshebeth (RV) (2 Sam 23:8; 1 Chron 11:11). His feat is that: "he lift up his spear against eight hundred, whom he slew at one time". How this man killed so many at on a single occasion we are not told. Did he drive them over a cliff? It is futile to speculate, but his incredible courage is top of the list.

We can think of the Lord's courage as He went to Calvary to take on Satan and his emissaries at the cross, "triumphing over them in it" (Col 2:15). How many enemies were slain at one time at Calvary?

How courageous are we? Or have we become mealy-mouthed as believers? It is one thing to be courageous in an area where we are not known, but what about where we work, or where we live, or within our family circle? We remember Daniel's courage in the court of Babylon, refusing to eat the king's meat or drink his wine (Daniel 1), or his three friends refusing to bow down to the idol (Daniel 3). We need to be bold in the school, university, office, or factory and never try to camouflage our Christianity. Courage will be rewarded: "them that honour me I will honour" (1 Sam 2:30).

The Lord will reward commitment in service

Eleazar was the next in the list (v 9). Interestingly, his mighty deed against the Philistines took place when all the other Israelites were retreating. It is not easy to take a stand when other Christians are withdrawing. Eleazar stood and fought alone with David in the barley field (1 Chron 11:13-14). How far would we go to defend our Lord? Eleazar stood and fought until his sword welded into his hand (v 10). He understood Paul's teaching to stand: "Wherefore take unto you the whole armour of God, that ye may be able to withstand in the evil day, and having done all, to stand" (Eph 6:13). His steadfast strength and complete commitment to the Lord has gone down in the eternal record as "mighty". "The Lord wrought a great victory that day", and God's people were rewarded due to Eleazer's commitment to divine things (v 10). Have we ever been blessed by the commitment of someone else? "Therefore, my beloved brethren, be ye steadfast, unmoveable, always abounding in the work of the Lord, forasmuch as ye know that your labour is not in vain in the Lord" (1 Cor 15:58). Moses' hands were steady to the going down of the sun (Ex 17:12). His commitment in prayer and intercession will not go unrewarded. Neither will ours.

The Lord was wearied with His journey. Night and day He prayed and preached. He was utterly committed to the will of His Father. Even when He was alone, He said, "and yet I am not alone, because the Father is with me" (John 16:32). Are we getting too comfortable? Does Bible study thrill us? Does worship excite us? Is soul winning our mission? Are we committed to the work of the Lord? One of the features of end times is a lack of commitment. In Malachi's day no one could even be bothered to tend to the doors of the House of God or maintain the fire on the altar (Mal 1:10). Let us be committed in the service of our Lord like Eleazar. The Lord values it.

The Lord values the cause and motivation of our service

The next man in the top "three" of the list is Shammah. Shammah defended a patch of lentils against the Philistines. The Philistines liked to fill wells (Gen 26) and starve God's people. Shammah stood against a troop of Philistines. Why? Because he reckoned that the field of lentils belonged to the Lord: "The land shall not be sold for ever: for the land is mine" (Lev 25:23). He believed that the land was given to Israel for God's glory, and that if Philistines took the land and brought in their idolatry there would be judgment: "That the land spue not you out also when ye defile it, as it spued out the nations that were before you" (Lev 18:28). He also knew that the field of lentils contained food for God's people.

How motivated are we to defend divine territory? Are we prepared to give ground on the truths like the Deity of Christ; the Sonship of Christ; the Headship of Christ, the Lordship of Christ; the holiness of His House? His Word feeds us as God's people, and a compromised position on the Word will result in stunted growth as Christians. The Lord said to the religious people of His day: "My house shall be called the house of prayer" (Matt 21:13). He would not give an inch of divine turf away on the truth of God's House. What is motivating us in the service of the Lord? We trust we all have a sense of the need to defend the "inheritance".

The Lord will reward consecration and devotion in service

The next three men in the list were rewarded for their sacrifice and devotion to David. David probably always had an elite force of thirty men. Thirty-four names are listed in the "30", but some died like Asahel and Uriah and would have been replaced so that at any given time David would have had 30 men. This might also explain the slightly larger list in 1 Chronicles 11 where there are 16 additional names. Perhaps 1 Chronicles 11 gives the list at the start of David's removal from Saul's palace, and the list in 2 Samuel 23 is during the days of his reign.

These three men simply heard David whisper his desire and it resulted in huge sacrifice (vv 13-17). They were consecrated to David's service and his wish was their command. Their devotion in breaking through a garrison of the Philistines to get David a drink of water from a well in Bethlehem broke David's heart and moved him to pour the water out as a drink offering to the Lord. Their sacrifice was regarded as an offering of worship. He would not dare drink the water.

How sensitive are we to the Saviour's desires? Or are we hard hearted even when He gives a clear command? How far would we go to serve Him? Would we be prepared to cross the sea? Can we really sing "Where He may lead me, I will go"? Would we take a job with a poorer salary in order to be freer for assembly gatherings? Would we be prepared to live in a poorer area if it was His will, or is where we live very important to us? Would we open our home to God's people?

We think of the consecration of Christ. The very heartbeat of the Father throbbed in time with His: "For even Christ pleased not himself; but, as it is written, the reproaches of them that reproached thee fell on me" (Rom 15:3). He took every insult to His Father as personal to Himself. He said, "... the cup which my Father hath given me, shall I not drink it?" (John 18:11). Surely His devotion inspires us all. Epaphroditus was so devoted to Paul on behalf of the Philippians that Paul said of him: "Receive him therefore in the Lord with all gladness; and hold such in reputation: Because for the work of Christ he was nigh unto death, not regarding his life" (Phil 2:29-30). May love for our Lord Jesus enflame us in His service.

The Lord will take into account context as He rewards service

Benaiah is one of the second group of three. What is interesting about his three feats of bravery is the unusual circumstances that surrounded them (vv 20-23). Others, for example, had killed lions but Benaiah killed a lion in a time of snow, in a pit. The weather was against him, the terrain was against him, nature was against him, but he had the Lord with him. He also was unarmed; he had only a staff and yet he took out an Egyptian mercenary who was armed with a spear. Perhaps others had accomplished greater or more public deeds, but Benaiah is recorded here because of the circumstances in which he carried out those feats, and as a result they were considered amazing.

There are those who may not get much notice from others, but the Lord will reward them highly for He knows that what they did was against the odds. He knew the battles they had to face at home, the wintry conditions they were up against. Others who stayed in sunnier climes might not have achieved half as much. The Lord will reward His people, taking their context into consideration.

Eliam (v 34) served David faithfully even if his father was Ahithophel, the man who betrayed David. David spoke of Ahithophel as, "mine own familiar friend, in whom I trusted, which did eat of my bread, hath lifted up his heel against me" (Ps 41:9). Therefore, David did not forget the background of Eliam's bravery and loyalty to him.

Ittai (v 29) was a Benjaminite, of Saul's' tribe, but David valued him greatly. God will reward those who serve Him against the odds. A Hittite is in the list (v 39), and an Ammonite (v 37), who were sworn enemies of God's people. They are all included. What grace! God will reward all such given the context of their service.

The Lord considered his mother even in the extremity of Calvary. Whether at an opportune time or not, He remembered to honour His mother. Paul exhorts us to preach in season and out of season. Timothy's father probably was not saved and was a Gentile, but Timothy began to preach to Jews. Peter was a simple fisherman and Luke was an able doctor, but Peter had the greater role. Paul was from Jewish, educated stock but was asked to live out of other people's homes. Jeremiah was asked not to have a wife; Ezekiel became a widower, and Hosea had a wife from a background of harlotry. All these servants will be rewarded for their service especially in the light of their circumstances.

The Lord will reward contentment in service

We read in verse 37 of Nahari "the Beerothite, armourbearer to Joab the son of Zeruiah". It is not everyone who is content to be simply the "armourbearer". It is not everyone who is prepared to play second fiddle. He simply walked in front of Joab and held his shield and served him. The Lord Jesus took the place of the servant saying:

"For whether is greater, he that sitteth at meat, or he that serveth? is not he that sitteth at meat? but I am among you as he that serveth" (Luke 22:27). The Lord Jesus became a carpenter. He was a despised Galilean. Are we willing to play a small role in the Assembly well? There will be a reward. Nahari's master, Joab, did not get the same reward. His name is missing from the list here. It is not how public our gift is that is rewarded but our commitment and contentment in the role we have been given. David was happy to be a message boy bringing his brothers bread and cheese (1 Sam 17:17-18) before he ever became King.

The Lord will reward character in service

The last name in the list is Uriah the Hittite (v 39). It must have been hard for David to write this name down given how terribly he had wronged Uriah (2 Sam 11). Is this the reason it was the last name on the list? And yet it was essential that the name was included. Uriah had refused to be a civilian when the people of God were at war with the Ammonites. He would not yield to David's offers to allow him to see his wife when there was a war on. And Uriah said unto David, "The ark, and Israel, and Judah, abide in tents; and my lord Joab, and the servants of my lord, are encamped in the open fields; shall I then go into mine house, to eat and to drink, and to lie with my wife? as thou livest, and as thy soul liveth, I will not do this thing (2 Sam 11:11). His character was intact even if the King encouraged him otherwise. Despite having the licence to take time off he would not. Even if he was given the green light His conscience told him the Lord knew better, and his character and reputation were intact as he slept outside rather than return to his house. He also was a mighty warrior who fought for the King. Our character in service will be blessed. As Paul writes to Timothy, "No man that warreth entangleth himself with the affairs of this life; that he may please him who hath chosen him to be a soldier" (2 Tim 2:4). Uriah is blessed for his character.

Joab is found in the list of mighty men in 1 Chronicles 11 (1 Chron

11:6, 10 "These also ..."). But he is deliberately omitted from the list here at the end of David's reign. Thirty-six names are given out of thirty-seven that are said to be listed (v 39), but one name is missing of the second group of three. Joab is missing as his character had been tarnished in relation to Absalom, Amasa and Abner, which all happened during the time of David's reign. He had become "chief and captain" in 1 Chronicles 11:6, but now he is no longer accepted. It is a sad reality that good people can go astray. Joab was skilful but not spiritual.

The Lord Jesus did the right things in the right manner and therefore had the moral authority to lead. He was meek and lowly of heart. He always did the right things in the right way with the right motive at the right time. At Calvary, He gave his back to the smiters and His cheeks to them that plucked off the hair (Isa 50:6), and even in a time of opposition showed His true character of compassion and righteousness. The Lord Jesus will reward those who display the character of Christ in their service.

The value of simplicity and dependency (Chapter 24)

The naming of the "mighty men" moves, sadly, to the numbering of the people. David had still to learn the true value of the really important things.

Simplicity

David's wanted a census. His motive for asking for a survey of the land seems to have been understood even by Joab: "And Joab said unto the king, Now the LORD thy God add unto the people, how many soever they be, an hundredfold, and that the eyes of my lord the king may see it: but why doth my lord the king delight in this thing?" (v 3). Against all advice David pursued this numbering agenda. On the face of it, it does not seem such a serious sin, but it ranks alongside his sin with Bathsheba. Why was he wanting the count? From verse nine it is obvious that he is assessing the strength of the army rather than taking a census of the people. Did he feel more secure when he knew how many there were in his army? Had he forgotten that in most of his battles that he won he was utterly outnumbered? Did he feel more able to think about how they could administer the need in the country when he knew all the numbers of the forces at his disposal? Had he forgotten that the first of his mighty men had killed 800 enemies at one time? Or did he overlook the fact that he had been preserved for years as a fugitive and that he had written, "I have been young, and now am old; yet have I not seen the righteous forsaken, nor his seed begging bread" (Ps 37:25). Had David reflected upon his own words this dreadful episode would have been avoided: "There is no king saved by the multitude of an host" (Ps 33:16). Was he boasting in the advance and size of the Kingdom in his reign? Had Samuel not taught him on the day of his anointing that "man looketh on the outward appearance, but the LORD looketh on the heart" (1 Sam 16:7)? Nathan's words to him from God on the day of receiving the Davidic covenant were: "Thus saith the LORD of hosts, I took thee from the sheepcote, from following the sheep, to be ruler over my people, over Israel" (2 Sam 7:8). God wants us to stay dependent, and is not interested in our bringing natural things into His Kingdom.

The world around us is still fixated with numbers - the size of the salary, house, car - and this can begin to affect us. We must take active steps, or we will think like the world. Even in spiritual things we can count numbers such how many attend a Christian conference, or count "gift" in the assembly, or make the number of people getting saved a matter for pride rather than a matter for thanksgiving and prayer. Our forefathers left the ornate cathedrals and the high churches to meet with a few people gathered round a loaf and cup in a house or a tin hall. This is blessed of God. Solomon wrote: "Better is little with the fear of the LORD than great treasure and trouble therewith" (Prov 15:16). May we learn the importance of valuing simplicity and simple dependency.

David's interest in numbers led to judgment. In fact, instead of an increase it led to a decrease. The sins associated with David – playing the fool in the Palace of Achish, the bringing up of the Ark on a cart, Bathsheba, and the numbering here happened at four diverse stages of David's life, and it reminds us that there are different temptations that will come our way at different times in our lives. We need to be on our guard. The issue of pride is a particular problem in old age.

Satan

We learn from 1 Chronicles 21:1 that Satan was behind the whole census notion. We might think we have good ideas but are they begotten by the flesh or by the Evil One? It is good to have clear Scripture for what we are doing, and a clear motive before the Lord. However, it was not until the deed had taken place that David's conscience smote him and he "said unto the LORD, I have sinned greatly in that I have done: and now, I beseech thee, O LORD, take away the iniquity of thy servant; for I have done very foolishly" (24:10). Satan loves it when God's people are intrigued by material and carnal things. Remember, "we wrestle ... against ... spiritual wickedness in high places" (Eph 6:12). We are not oblivious to his techniques: beware "Lest Satan should get an advantage of us: for we are not ignorant of his devices" (2 Cor 2:11). We must "resist [him] stedfast in the faith" (1 Pet 5:9), and he can be overcome: "Resist the devil, and he will flee from you" (James 4:7).

Sovereign hand of God

But God was behind it all too (2 Sam 24:1). He permitted it but Satan suggested it and provoked it. The occasion became the opportunity not only for God to show David his sin but also to judge people for a variety of other sins not known to us. David wanted the number of the people to increase, but 70,000 died! How solemn. David then had to choose between famine, war, or pestilence as a punishment for his action. He chose pestilence as he wanted to be shut up to God's mercy (24:13-14). A wise choice! He pleaded for the sheep that he genuinely cared for, and the judgment was cut short (24:17). It is good when we can recognise that we have sinned.

Sacrifice and the sanctuary

It is into this scene that one of David's greatest acts take place - he purchases Zion. He acquires the threshing floor and the oxen and the implements for 50 shekels of silver, and later he purchases the whole Temple Mount for 600 shekels of gold (1 Chron 29:2-3; 22:14; 21:25). He sacrifices at great cost, and refuses to offer a sacrifice for nothing: "... neither will I offer burnt offerings unto the LORD my God of that which doth cost me nothing" (2 Sam 24:24). David knows intuitively that it is the House of God. He said, "This is the house of the LORD God, and this is the altar of burnt offering for Israel" (1 Chron 22:1). The man who had brought the Ark to Jerusalem, and had the foresight to make Jerusalem the capital, now sees that Mount Moriah is the place where God's House should be built. Indeed, the House of God was already there long before Solomon built the temple. God's presence was there. It is at the moment when the judgment stops that the blessing begins. David will now spend all his efforts providing and contributing to God's House.

True worth is always found at the place of sacrifice. We learn the correct significance of things at the cross; there our ego, our education, our achievements, our material possessions are nothing. David paid the full price for the place of sacrifice, and so did our blessed Lord at the cross. It is here that nothing else matters, the cross eclipses the world's treasures: "God forbid that I should glory, save in the cross of our Lord Jesus Christ, by whom the world is crucified unto me, and I unto the world" (Gal 6:14).

PSALM 29

[A Psalm of David.]

[1] Give unto the LORD, O ye mighty, give unto the LORD glory and strength.

[2] Give unto the LORD the glory due unto his name; worship the LORD in the beauty of holiness.

[3] The voice of the LORD is upon the waters: the God of glory thundereth: the LORD is upon many waters.

[4] The voice of the LORD is powerful; the voice of the LORD is full of majesty.

[5] The voice of the LORD breaketh the cedars; yea, the LORD breaketh the cedars of Lebanon.

[6] He maketh them also to skip like a calf; Lebanon and Sirion like a young unicorn.

[7] The voice of the LORD divideth the flames of fire.

[8] The voice of the LORD shaketh the wilderness; the LORD shaketh the wilderness of Kadesh.

[9] The voice of the LORD maketh the hinds to calve, and discovereth the forests: and in his temple doth every one speak of his glory.

[10] The LORD sitteth upon the flood; yea, the LORD sitteth King for ever.

[11] The LORD will give strength unto his people; the LORD will bless his people with peace.

CHAPTER 19

David: His Charge

1 Kings 1-2

David is now an old frail man who needs to be kept warm and nursed, but he still has incredible strength of faith. His forty-year reign is ending, and we see the anointing of Solomon at the King's command, and the solemn charge to Solomon by David. During this time, the rebellion by Adonijah is brought to a swift end. An orderly handover of power takes place when David is still alive. We learn in these sections about the importance of good transitions, the trials of old age, the blessings that an older generation can give us as well as the burdens that can be passed on intergenerationally.

Weakness of body

The opening four verses of 1 Kings describe an old, frail King David. He is so old that he needs to be kept warm and has a full-time nurse in Abishag. It is expressly clear from verse 4 that Abishag was a nurse and not a wife or a concubine. The principle of looking after people when they are older is relevant for us today and was clearly expected of the early church (see, for example, the instruction about widows in 1 Timothy 5).

Worthiness in old age

There is something sad that the boy who was so full of vigour with his "ruddy" countenance in 1 Samuel 16 is now so weak. Does Solomon remember this about his father when he describes old age so vividly in Ecclesiastes chapter 12? And yet David had lived a full life with so much to look back on with thankfulness. The Chronicle account says that David "died in a good old age, full of days, riches, and honour" (1 Chron 29:28). This is a beautiful description of David in his last few days. Weakness of body did not mean failure but an occasion for thanksgiving that God had given him such a full and good life. It is also true to say that David's faith was strong in death as the narrative in these chapters clearly shows. He, like the Apostle Paul, "kept the faith" and "fought a good fight". The testimony of the Holy Spirit to David through Paul is: "David, after he had served his own generation by the will of God, fell on sleep" (Acts 13:36). Solomon knew that David was also interested in the next generation as well as his own, and much later Solomon would write that "the beauty of old men is the grey head" (Prov 20:29). It is good when we can see past bodily weakness and revere the wisdom of old age.

Wrong assumptions

The reason why David's physical frailty is emphasised in the account in 1 Kings is because of the context of an uprising by Adonijah (1:5). Adonijah waited until his father was very weak and then said, "I will be king". We need to watch out for people who say, "I will", and want to lord it "over God's heritage" (1 Peter 5:3). They very often wait till weak moments in assembly life before they make their move. Adonijah possibly thought that because three of his brothers had died, and that he was now "officially" the oldest in the family, it was his "right" to be king (2 Sam 3:4). We can have ideas in our head about our "rights" in the assembly that have no basis in Scripture. We ought to carefully guard the assumptions we make as they can lead to tragic outcomes. The succession plan for David has been established by God in Solomon (1 Chron 28:9, 11, 20; 29:1, 19). Adonijah knows this and yet organises a bodyguard of fifty men and arranges a lavish feast for the king's sons to mark his coronation (1 Kings 1:5-11) whilst studiously avoiding inviting Solomon and those close to David (v 10).

Warped reasoning

Perhaps surprisingly, Adonijah appears to have the blessing of Joab and Abiathar (1:7) as he agitates to be the next king. We do not know why Abiathar joins with Adonijah and against David, but there were consequences. As result, Abiathar's seed, which were already severely reduced by the cruel action of Doeg the Edomite (1 Sam 22), are removed from active priestly service by Solomon (1 Kings 2:27). This was prophesied by Samuel to Eli so many years before. Instead, Zadok the priest, who remained faithful to David, is used and his offspring will one day function in the Millennial temple (Ezek 44:15).

Perhaps Joab, who has remained loyal to David all the way through, finds intolerable the idea that a son of Bathsheba is to sit on the throne after David. Sadly, therefore, at the end of a life of loyalty to David he rebels against him. We must remember that the child Solomon, produced by the marriage of David and Bathsheba, had committed no wrong. We dare not lay the sin of the parents at the door of the children and treat them badly. However, it was the Lord that was behind Solomon sitting upon the throne and it was not a succession plan devised by David. Sometimes we must acknowledge the sovereign hand of God in giving someone a particular role.

Adonijah may have used the excuse of the substandard parenting of David for an explanation as to why he was used to getting his own way (1:6). Joab may have been able to justify his rebellion because of his revulsion of David's sin with Bathsheba for opposing Solomon. Abiathar might have felt that Zadok was getting too much place and so sided with Adonijah. People can have diverse and often personal reasons for getting involved in a coup. Nevertheless, however they may have justified their actions, all three of these men were sinning. There are lessons here for us as we must be before the Lord about our motivation for the choices we make in life and not use the failures of others as an excuse for moving outside of the revealed mind of God.

Wise actions

We need to be on our guard at these critical moments when good men are passing on. Thankfully, Nathan the prophet, who has been faithful to David for so long, acts decisively. He tells Bathsheba that she must go in to see David and make him aware of Adonijah's actions

- his lavish feast, his claim to be king, the usurpation of Joab and Abiathar, and the exclusion of Solomon. Bathsheba must also remind David that he had told her that Solomon was to be King. She obeys this instruction and Nathan wisely shores up Bathsheba's testimony by his own presence and evidence (vv 11-27). He does this privately so that David does not think he is simply repeating Bathsheba's words. Even in days of weakness and failure, the testimony of two is required (Deut 17:6). Much damage has been done when people act on a prejudiced story. David might have wondered if Bathsheba was exaggerating, given it was her son that was under attack. Therefore, Nathan's role in confirming the story is crucial.

This joint intervention results in David acting decisively (vv 28-51). It is lovely to see his concern for the Kingdom right up until his dying day. David gives instructions that Solomon is to be taken on David's own mule to the Gihon (a spring just outside the city of Jerusalem) and that he is to be accompanied by Benaiah and all the men of war. He is then to be anointed King that very day at the Gihon by Zadok the priest and Nathan the prophet, and the trumpets must blow to announce that Solomon is king. These actions all happened immediately, and the city rang with the news of Solomon's reign. Decisive actions are sometimes needed to stem the tide of evil. The coronation of Solomon stops the usurpation of Adonijah in its tracks as the guests creep away in fear (v 49). The old weak man David acts in faith and in power at the very end. The Kingdom is more important than his own person, and he does everything he can to ensure a smooth transition of rule. Would that all leaders had the same wisdom.

Parting words (1 Kings 2:1-10)

The "overlap" period seems to be very short and David is now going the "way of all the earth" (2:2). He has some parting advice to the young King Solomon as he takes the reigns of the Kingdom.

David charges Solomon to "be ... strong" (v 2). David, himself, is passing on, but dangerous people are still alive, for example Joab, Shimei. Abiathar, Adonijah. The Kingdom is not secure. David gives this charge to Solomon to strengthen him. This was the Lord's encouragement to Joshua: "Be strong and of a good courage" (Josh 1:6). The task that was ahead of Solomon was a huge one and he would require strength of character. That strength would come from the Lord. Paul exhorts the Ephesians to "be strong (or better 'be strengthened') in the Lord, and in the power of his might" (Eph 6:10).

David encourages Solomon to "shew thyself a man" (v 2), to demonstrate his courage and take the Kingdom seriously. This is not just macho talk. David knows that Solomon will have very difficult decisions to take and not all of them will be popular. He wants him to rise to the occasion, show integrity, and demonstrate his ability to take decisions in the fear of God.

The secret to the success of Solomon's Kingdom is in his knowledge of, and obedience to, the Scriptures. David urges Solomon to "keep his (the Lord's) statutes, and his commandments, and his judgments, and his testimonies" (v 3). He uses key technical words to describe the Scriptures. The statutes are the broad boundaries and definitions of Scripture about how we ought to behave; the commandments are the specific prohibitions or exhortations that we must live by; the judgments are actions which must be carried out, including restitution. Obedience to God's word was the secret to prosperity and a happy life, "that thou mayest prosper in all that thou doest, and whithersoever thou turnest thyself" (v 3).

David reminds Solomon of the continuance of the Kingdom. He says, "That the LORD may continue his word which he spake concerning me, saying, If thy children take heed to their way, to walk before me in truth ..." (v 4). God had promised to bless the Kingdom through David's seed, even to the bringing in of the Messiah. The Kingdom is eternal. However, that did not mean that David's seed could disobey God's word and God would not act. God could temporarily suspend the Kingdom which he did some 400 years later, using Babylon to remove them for seventy years. It was incumbent, therefore, that Solomon's family also revered the word of God. He must teach it to his sons and daughters because God said that "If thy children ... walk before me in truth with all their heart and with all their soul, there shall not fail thee (said he) a man on the throne of Israel" (v 4).

David knows that Solomon will be required to maintain righteous standards in the Kingdom. He knows there is an issue that he had failed to deal with, and it is this that he encourages Solomon to address: "Moreover thou knowest also what Joab the son of Zeruiah did to me" (v 5). David reminds him of the murder of Abner and Amasa and encourages him to find a way to ensure that justice is served. There was an open admission of David's failure here and an encouragement for Solomon to act righteously. As David said himself, "He that ruleth over men must be just" (2 Sam 23:3).

David also knows that the Kingdom will only prosper if it is marked by love and compassion. He exhorts Solomon to "shew kindness unto the sons of Barzillai ... and let them be of those that eat at thy table" (v 7). He recalls the high moments of his Kingdom when he showed kindness to others like Mephibosheth. He knows that Solomon's Kingdom will be maintained by the free will offerings of others. As an example, he reminds him of Barzillai who supported David all his life even in the distressing days when Absalom rebelled. He reminds Solomon to look after Barzillai's family as a perpetual reminder to him of the need to be supportive to others, and as a fulfilment to a promise he made to Barzillai. Solomon listened to David and would later write: "Thine own friend, and thy father's friend, forsake not" (Prov 27:10).

Finally, David knows that there are many quandaries that Solomon will have to face. He says, "for thou art a wise man, and knowest what thou oughtest to do" (v 9). One problem is a man called Shimei whom David vowed not to kill. David reminds Solomon that this vow would be null and void at his death and then Solomon must use his wisdom to deal with Shimei, reminding him of the evil character that he displayed.

After this seven-stranded "charge" by David, he "slept with his fathers" (v 10). This expression simply means he moved into the place of the dead. David's pilgrimage came to an end. The remarkable and great man had many times anticipated the day when he would be in heavenly glory and behold the very face of God. That day had arrived as it will for us all. He had now come into the good of his own Psalm: "As for me, I will behold thy face in righteousness: I shall be satisfied, when I awake, with thy likeness" (Ps 17:15).

PSALM 72

[A Psalm for Solomon.]

¹ Give the king thy judgments, O God, and thy righteousness unto the king's son.

² He shall judge thy people with righteousness, and thy poor with judgment.

³ The mountains shall bring peace to the people, and the little hills, by righteousness.

⁴ He shall judge the poor of the people, he shall save the children of the needy, and shall break in pieces the oppressor.

⁵ They shall fear thee as long as the sun and moon endure, throughout all generations.

⁶ He shall come down like rain upon the mown grass: as showers that water the earth.

⁷ In his days shall the righteous flourish; and abundance of peace so long as the moon endureth.

⁸ He shall have dominion also from sea to sea, and from the river unto the ends of the earth.

⁹ They that dwell in the wilderness shall bow before him; and his enemies shall lick the dust.

¹⁰ The kings of Tarshish and of the isles shall bring presents: the kings of Sheba and Seba shall offer gifts.

¹¹ Yea, all kings shall fall down before him: all nations shall serve him.

¹² For he shall deliver the needy when he crieth; the poor also, and him that hath no helper.

¹³ He shall spare the poor and needy, and shall save the souls of the needy.

¹⁴ He shall redeem their soul from deceit and violence: and precious shall their blood be in his sight.

¹⁵ And he shall live, and to him shall be given of the gold of Sheba: prayer also shall be made for him continually; and daily shall he be praised.

¹⁶ There shall be an handful of corn in the earth upon the top of the mountains; the fruit thereof shall shake like Lebanon: and they of the city shall flourish like grass of the earth.

¹⁷ His name shall endure for ever: his name shall be continued as long as the sun: and men shall be blessed in him: all nations shall call him blessed.

¹⁸ Blessed be the LORD God, the God of Israel, who only doeth wondrous things.

¹⁹ And blessed be his glorious name for ever: and let the whole earth be filled with his glory; Amen, and Amen.

²⁰ The prayers of David the son of Jesse are ended.

CHAPTER 20

David: His Contribution and Conclusion

1 Chronicles 23-29; 2 Samuel 22-23:1-7

We have reached the end of our travels with this incredible man, David. What a remarkable contribution he made to the furtherance of God's Kingdom! The Chronicle account tends to detail his impact in terms of wealth accumulated for the Temple, and the account in 2 Samuel 23 focuses on his words, indeed his "last words", which he has left us. David gave Solomon a tremendous legacy for the House of God and the Word of God. It is within these two spheres that David's contribution is really known and will be known eternally. The Chronicler lists for us the gold, silver, precious stones, priestly order, singers, instruments, and porters that David provided for the House of God. His wise sayings in these "last words" (2 Sam 23:1) are a reminder of David's vast contribution to the Word of God, for example his 75 psalms. Our own hearts are challenged as we review the life of David and see a man after God's own heart, a unique accolade for a remarkable man and an incredible life.

His psalms

David wrote half of the Psalter. Seventy-three of his Psalms have the title "A Psalm of David" or equivalent, and another two Psalms, (Psalms 2 and 95) are attributed to David by the Spirit of God in the New Testament (Acts 4:25; Heb 4:7). Psalm 3 is the first Psalm of David in the Psalter, and it is written at the time of Absalom's rebellion, so we discover that David's Psalms are not organised chronologically but thematically throughout the five books of Psalms. Thirteen of the Psalm titles include details of their settings, and these Psalms are all arranged chronologically in this book after the relevant portion has been discussed.

This incredible song book for Israel is a huge contribution by David to the Word of God. He also composed music, made musical instruments, and gave instruction about how these Psalms were to be sung. Even many generations later, Hezekiah in his day "set the Levites in the house of the LORD with cymbals, with psalteries, and with harps, according to the commandment of David ... And the Levites stood with the instruments of David ... And when the burnt offering began, the song of the LORD began also with the trumpets, and with the instruments ordained by David king of Israel" (2 Chron 29:25-27). Thousands of years later David's Psalms are still being sung. In fact, the Lord Jesus stated that, "my words shall not pass away" (Matt 24:35), and so these Psalms are ancient but also eternal.

How many a saint has been supported, strengthened and inspired by the Psalms of David? His experiences with God are authentic, borne out of real and often raw issues. His pain is as much a legacy as his praise. We have quoted John Douglas from Ashgill, Scotland, already but it bears repeating: "If David's heart had ne'er been wrung, then David's psalms had ne'er been sung". His pen has helped millions, more than his sword ever did. Centuries later, Paul reminds the Colossian believers: "Let the word of Christ dwell in you richly in all wisdom; teaching and admonishing one another in psalms and hymns and spiritual songs, singing with grace in your hearts to the Lord" (Col 3:16).

His proverbs or prophetic wise sayings

At the end of his life, David, in his "last words" gives us some wise prophetic sayings in 2 Samuel 23 which may have been put to song, and they certainly give us an insight as to how he saw his contribution to God's Word. He commenced by saying, "Now these be the last words of David. David the son of Jesse said, and the man who was raised up on high, the anointed of the God of Jacob, and the sweet psalmist of Israel, said ..." (v 1). Firstly, David never lost sight of the fact that he was simply a son of Jesse who had been raised up. He never forgot where he came from. Secondly, he never forgot that it was God who anointed him and not so much the prophet Samuel. He recognised God's sovereignty. David's reference to the "the God of Jacob", and not "the God of Israel" suggests that he, like Jacob, had been preserved in difficult days, had weaknesses, yet was chosen by God to lead His people. This title of God is another reminder to us that David did not think of himself other than as an object of grace. This is an attitude we must all adopt.

David tells us that the words that he contributed were by revelation, inspired by the Holy Spirit: "The spirit of the LORD spake by me, and his word was in my tongue" (v 2). So, we need to treat God's Word reverently. The Scriptures are genuinely hot with the breath of God (2 Tim 3:16).

David also taught us something of the character of God: "The God of Israel said, the Rock of Israel spake to me, He that ruleth over men must be just, ruling in the fear of God" (v 3). The righteous God demands righteousness. Therefore, we need to ensure that our lives are responding to God's Word, and that we move with fear, in holy awe, and act in harmony with His character.

God's Word, when obeyed, leads to refreshment like the dawn of a new day or as the green shoots of grass after rain: "And he shall be as the light of the morning, when the sun riseth, even a morning without clouds; as the tender grass springing out of the earth by clear shining after rain" (v 4). Vitality and energy originate in God's Word. How often has a company of Christians found encouragement and renewed joy by a word given in due season. The Scriptures revive us.

Furthermore, David told us that God's Word gives us reassurance of recovery: "For does not my house stand so with God? For he has made with me an everlasting covenant, ordered in all things and secure. For will he not cause to prosper all my help and my desire?" (v 5; ESV). We know that God's Word is true and will come to pass. This gives great comfort and assurance. David revelled in the covenant promise given to him in 2 Samuel 7 concerning his house and the Kingdom. On his death bed he knew that God keeps His covenants. God's Word brings comfort.

Finally, he warned that there will be retribution to all who oppose the Lord: "But the sons of Belial shall be all of them as thorns thrust away, because they cannot be taken with hands: But the man that shall touch them must be fenced with iron and the staff of a spear; and they shall be utterly burned with fire in the same place" (vv 6-7). David has much to tell us here in his "last words" about the place of God's Word and the authority that it contains for all of us and especially for those who take a lead amongst God's people.

His pattern for the House of God

David not only contributed to the Word of God, but he gave Solomon the pattern for the House of God. "Then David gave to Solomon his son the pattern of the porch, and of the houses thereof, and of the treasuries thereof, and of the upper chambers thereof, and of the inner parlours thereof, and of the place of the mercy seat ...". he pattern he gave to Solomon was from God which he had received directly by the Holy Spirit: "... And the pattern of all that he had by the spirit, of the courts of the house of the LORD, and of all the chambers round about, of the treasuries of the house of God, and of the treasuries of the dedicated things" (1 Chron 28:11-12). Moses had a visual pattern (Ex 25:9, 40), but David had a written pattern: "All this, said David, the LORD made me understand in writing by his hand upon me, even all the works of this pattern" (1 Chron 28:19). Solomon would not have been at liberty to change this pattern as it came directly from God. However, he was fully supported by David in building the House to the pattern.

We cannot tamper with God's pattern that He has set out in the New Testament for His House (for example Matt 18:20; Acts 2:41-42; 1 Cor 11). God's House today is not a material building but the gathering together of God's people to the Name of the Lord Jesus. Paul delivered this legacy to Timothy and wanted him to pass it on intact to others: "And the things that thou hast heard of me among many witnesses, the same commit thou to faithful men, who shall be able to teach others also" (2 Tim 2:2). Paul wanted "the same" to be passed on, undiluted and undiminished. Just as with Solomon, we are not at liberty to add to the pattern.

His provision for the House of God

David provided the servants (1 Chron 23-24), the singers (1 Chron 25), and the stewards (porters and the treasurers - 1 Chron 26). He also supplied the supervisors (1 Chron 27), and the silver, gold and brass (1 Chron 28-29). David thought of everything, but he did say to Solomon that he could "add thereto" (1 Chron 22:14). This is an encouragement and a reminder to us that our contribution is always welcome in God's House.

The provision David gave for the House is colossal by any estimation: "Now, behold, in my trouble I have prepared for the house of the LORD an hundred thousand talents of gold, and a thousand thousand talents of silver; and of brass and iron without weight; for it is in abundance: timber also and stone have I prepared; and thou mayest add thereto" (1 Chron 22:14). At the time of writing, one talent of gold would be worth over 14 million pounds. Therefore, conservative calculations put the weight of gold and silver that David laid up for the House of God to be in the categories of multiple billions of pounds in today's money. No expense was spared. What does the House of God mean to us? What are we contributing?

His prayer for the House of God

David feels his insignificance and unworthiness as he prays for the House of God saying, "But who am I, and what is my people, that we should be able to offer so willingly after this sort? ..." (1 Chron 29:14-15). This is the attitude that all must adopt who pray in God's House. David recognises that all that he has done for the House of God, and all that God's people are offering willingly, really comes from God in the first place: "O LORD our God, all this store that we have prepared to build thee an house for thine holy name cometh of thine hand, and is all thine own ... and now have I seen with joy thy people, which are present here, to offer willingly unto thee" (1 Chron 29:16-17). David is convinced that if God's people are to be blessed in God's House they will need to prepare their hearts and ensure that God's Word is paramount: "O LORD God of Abraham, Isaac, and of Israel, our fathers, keep this for ever in the imagination of the thoughts of the heart of thy people, and prepare their heart unto thee: And give unto Solomon my son a perfect heart, to keep thy commandments, thy testimonies, and thy statutes and to do all these things, and to build the palace, for the which I have made provision" (1 Chron 29:18-19).

Are we contributing to the collective prayers of God's people for His House? Paul gives specific instruction about the prayer meeting to Timothy in 1 Timothy 2. He, like David, felt the great vulnerability of God's House and the essential requirement for prayer. The legacy that David left was his prayer life, and, of course, so many of his prayers, like those of Paul, are recorded in Scripture.

His praise for the House of God

The praise of David and the rejoicing as Solomon is crowned King seem to merge in the Chronicle account: "And David said to all the congregation, Now bless the LORD your God. And all the congregation blessed the LORD God of their fathers, and bowed down their heads, and worshipped the LORD, and the king. And they sacrificed sacrifices unto the LORD, and offered burnt offerings unto the LORD, on the morrow after that day, even a thousand bullocks, a thousand rams, and a thousand lambs, with their drink offerings, and sacrifices in abundance for all Israel: And did eat and drink before the LORD on that day with great gladness. And they made Solomon the son of David king the second time, and anointed him unto the LORD to be the chief governor, and Zadok to be priest (1 Chron 29:20-22).

The link between the House and the Kingdom, between the Priest and the King is established. David can look forward to a day when a "greater than Solomon" (Matt 12:42) would reign over the whole world and stand on the very turf where the House of God was erected by Solomon: "and of his kingdom there shall be no end" (Luke 1:33).

His parting

David the young shepherd boy from Bethlehem, now "died in a good old age, full of days, riches, and honour: and Solomon his son reigned in his stead" (1 Chron 29:28). His long reign of forty years has ended. What a legacy he has left us. What a contribution to God's Word and God's House. What hope he has given us in our trials, what comfort he gives us by his restoration. We have also learned from his life pitfalls to avoid. But the prevailing touch from David is to our hearts, inducing us to worship. He presents to us pictures of the Saviour and leaves for us the prospect of a future Kingdom for Israel where Christ, the Son of David, will reign for ever.

God said of David that he was, "a man after mine own heart" (Acts 13:22). That is said of no one else. There were features in the heart of David that corresponded to the deepest yearnings of the heart of God. The Bible is full of references to David. The last mention in the Bible is so instructive: "I Jesus have sent mine angel to testify unto you these things in the churches. I am the root and the offspring of David, and the bright and morning star" (Rev 22:16). We feel sure that the whole reason for the record of David's life is to turn our eyes to his Greater Son, the Lord Jesus. Amen.

PSALM 30

[A Psalm and Song at the dedication of the house of David.]

¹ I will extol thee, O LORD; for thou hast lifted me up, and hast not made my foes to rejoice over me.

² O LORD my God, I cried unto thee, and thou hast healed me.

³ O LORD, thou hast brought up my soul from the grave: thou hast kept me alive, that I should not go down to the pit.

⁴ Sing unto the LORD, O ye saints of his, and give thanks at the remembrance of his holiness.

⁵ For his anger endureth but a moment; in his favour is life: weeping may endure for a night, but joy cometh in the morning.

⁶ And in my prosperity I said, I shall never be moved.

⁷ LORD, by thy favour thou hast made my mountain to stand strong: thou didst hide thy face, and I was troubled.

⁸ I cried to thee, O LORD; and unto the LORD I made supplication.

⁹ What profit is there in my blood, when I go down to the pit? Shall the dust praise thee? shall it declare thy truth?

¹⁰ Hear, O LORD, and have mercy upon me: LORD, be thou my helper.

¹¹ Thou hast turned for me my mourning into dancing: thou hast put off my sackcloth, and girded me with gladness;

¹² To the end that my glory may sing praise to thee, and not be silent. O LORD my God, I will give thanks unto thee for ever.